TWAYNE'S WORLD AUTHORS SERIES

A Survey of the World's Literature

Sylvia E. Bowman, Indiana University

GENERAL EDITOR

SWEDEN

Leif Sjöberg, Columbia University

EDITOR

Ingmar Bergman

(*TWAS 32*)

TWAYNE'S WORLD AUTHORS SERIES (TWAS)

The purpose of TWAS is to survey the major writers —novelists, dramatists, historians, poets, philosophers, and critics—of the nations of the world. Among the national literatures covered are those of Australia, Canada, China, Eastern Europe, France, Germany, Greece, India, Italy, Japan, Latin America, New Zealand, Poland, Russia, Scandinavia, Spain, and the African nations, as well as Hebrew, Yiddish, and Latin Classical literatures. This survey is complemented by Twayne's United States Authors Series and English Authors Series.

The intent of each volume in these series is to present a critical-analytical study of the works of the writer; to include biographical and historical material that may be necessary for understanding, appreciation, and critical appraisal of the writer; and to present all material in clear, concise English—but not to vitiate the scholarly content of the work by doing so.

Ingmar Bergman

By BIRGITTA STEENE
Temple University

Twayne Publishers, Inc.   ::   New York

Finally the public will demand the film of imagination, of vision. And then will come the day of the poet, the scenario-writer, or whatever we are to call him. For actually this artist will be a new type of artist —an artist with the visual sensibility of the painter, the vision of the poet, and the time-sense of the musician.

HERBERT READ

The completion of this study has been facilitated by the generous assistance of librarians and other personnel at the Swedish Film Institute in Stockholm and by a grant from the Swedish Institute for Cultural Exchange Abroad. My special thanks to Rune Waldecrantz and Jean Alexander, who have read the manuscript in full and made many valuable suggestions.

Preface

It may seem strange to include a man who is best known as a maker of motion pictures in a world authors series, and many cinematic purists would no doubt object, using as their main argument that the film is not words but image, a visual art in which the written scenario is no more than an artistic outline or first draft. Some Swedish critics have approached Bergman's films with the gallant understanding that their verbal content is largely irrelevant, or they have accused Ingmar Bergman of displaying literary ambitions in an art form where these do not belong. Harry Schein's statement apropos of *The Seventh Seal* may be taken as representative of this kind of critique: "Ingmar Bergman creates in an intimately visual style. Unfortunately, he does not trust his visual power of expression sufficiently. Where nothing is missing, he adds the word, not the simple word but the literary word."[1]

In 1948 a collection of Bergman's plays for the theater appeared in print. But a second volume was turned down by his publisher, and it may be nothing but sour grapes that have made Bergman frequently deny that he is an author. In his introduction to the American edition of four of his screenplays, he writes: "I myself have never had any ambitions to be an author. I do not want to write novels, short stories, essays, biographies, or even plays for the theater. I only want to make films. . . . I am a film-maker, not an author."[2]

In the diary he kept while assisting Bergman during the shooting of *Winter Light*, Vilgot Sjöman mentions Ingmar Bergman's dislike for the intellectual writer who works by means of psychological analysis and philosophical argument.[3] Bergman seems to associate this type of writer with all authors of fiction and poetry. They work with great discipline and consciousness, while those who create intuitively are the playwrights. Bergman once dismissed a "charge" that he was a writer with the argument that he worked "entirely spontaneously. I vomited forth what I brooded over without bothering about the aesthetic qualities. The words stood absolutely naked. A dramatist cannot hide himself in word-magic like a novelist or a poet."[4]

The introduction to the American edition of *Four Screenplays* includes a statement by Bergman on how he conceives a film:

A film for me begins with something very vague—a chance remark or a bit of conversation, a hazy but agreeable event unrelated to any particular situation. It can be a few bars of music, a shaft of light across the street. . . . These are split-second impressions that disappear as quickly as they come, yet leave behind a mood like pleasant dreams.[5] It is a mental state, not an actual story, but one abounding in fertile associations and images. Most of all, it is a brightly colored thread sticking out of the dark sack of the unconscious. . . . This primitive nucleus strives to achieve a definite form, moving in a way that may be lazy and half asleep at first. Its stirring is accompanied by vibrations and rhythms, which are very special and unique to each film. The picture sequences then assume a pattern in accordance with these rhythms, obeying laws born out of and conditioned by my original stimulus.[6]

The interesting thing about this rendering of the creative process is that it is quite similar to Henry James' description of the embryonic growth of one of his short stories or novels. As Lionel Trilling has pointed out, Bergman's statement does not serve to substantiate his belief in his non-literariness: "The process he describes would seem to be the process of artistic conception in general—or at least of modern artistic conception in general —and if the composer of music (to whom Mr. Bergman says the film-maker has the closest affinity) or the painter would assent to it, so too would the poet or the short story writer and perhaps even the novelist."[7]

But if Bergman's statement about his way of composing a film does not show him as devoid of the literary impulse as he claims, it is also true that only a small part of the process he describes can be expressed verbally: "The only thing that can be satisfactorily transferred from that original complex of rhythms and moods is the dialogue, and even dialogue is a sensitive substance which may offer resistance. Written dialogue is like a musical score, almost incomprehensible to the average person." [8]

The declaration of independence from literature that Bergman makes is as old as the film art itself. The prominent Russian film theorist and director Sergei Eisenstein was quite contemptuous of literary dependence, not only for the screen art but also for the art of the theater. To him it was correct to borrow plots from literary works but no method or technique. This was also the approach of Mauritz Stiller and Victor Sjöström, the two classic directors in the Swedish cinema, who borrowed several of Selma Lagerlöf's stories for film plots but showed little reverence for the original conception. It brought Stiller, in particular, into great arguments with the authoress; one of her letters to him criticizes his handling of her literary works; at the same time, however, it foreshadows the importance of having scripts written exclusively for the screen:

. . . Now when I see that you consider that the book should only be a source of inspiration and that the contents should be changed to something quite new, exclusively meant for the film, then I must honestly say that I can no longer agree with you. . . . I understand that you, with your great ability, are trying to raise the film to something artistic, a new branch of art, like music to the eye, if I may say so. But in order to do this it certainly is necessary that the story be meant for the film from the beginning.[9]

The tension between fiction and the new screen art was intensified with the introduction of sound. Violent protests against spoken dialogue arose from the supporters of the cinema. Paul Rotha, the director, declared in 1930 that the sound picture would never destroy "the original and highest form of cinema, the silent, flat film with synchronized or orchestra accompaniment, which is indisputably the most effective medium for the conveyance of the dramatic content of a theme to the mind of an audience." [10] The year before, J. G. Fletcher had categorically dismissed the possibilities which might reside in the combination of visual and audible elements: "A complete boycott of 'talking films' should be the first duty of anyone who has ever achieved a moment's pleasure from the contemplation of any film." [11]

Even contemporary playwrights came to the support of the cinema purists. Luigi Pirandello declared: "The cinema must free itself of literature, leaving narrative to novels and the theater. It should steep itself in music. I refer to that kind of music which can speak to everyone without the addition of any words and for which cinematography can become the visual medium. Thus I would say, pure music and pure image." [12] Pirandello coined a word for this new art form: *Cinemelography*, the visible language of sound. He has found a disciple of sorts in Ingmar Bergman, who has often noted the relationship between pictorial image and music. In an interview in *The Saturday Review* he said: "I find it easier to compare film . . . to music. In pure film and pure music there is a feeling that goes directly to some deeper level of the listener or viewer, and only afterward is it possible to analyze the experience." [13]

It may seem like a strange paradox that in spite of Bergman's denial of film as literature and in spite of their own low opinion of him as a writer, critics have usually taken a "literary" approach to his work. One reason for this may be the recurrence in Bergman's films of a set of dramatic motifs, the totality of which forms a personal philosophy or vision and easily lends itself to thematic analyses that resemble some of the methods used in literary criticism. Another reason could be Bergman's dependence upon a dramatic story. His characters may at times lack dramatic reality and be abstracted to the point where they move along as symbols or conceptual images, but they are almost always involved in a plot of great dramatic potential. And as Lionel Trilling has argued, "as long as the cinema makes use of story, it is captive to the concepts that control story in literature." [14]

A third and crucial reason for the literary approach to Bergman's films lies in the existence of printed screenplays where Bergman makes no attempt to include technical references to the actual shooting of a film. The published version of his work contains no "montageship," to use the jargon of the movie-maker. Quite on the contrary, Bergman often adds long descriptive passages, including metaphors of smell and color, which cannot be transmitted to the screen (with one exception, Bergman has made only black-and-white films). As Pauline Kael has pointed out in her review of the pocket edition of *Four Screenplays*, the "scripts" are a sort of hybrid between a play and a novel, and they can be read as dramatic literature: "They resemble plays that have discarded the classic unities." [15]

Preface

There is the same good reason for paying attention to the text of Bergman's screenplays as there is for reading Shakespeare: some things become clarified in a close study of the dialogue. At the same time, however, a Shakespeare play can only be fully appreciated when produced on the stage. A Bergman script may be autonomous, but it becomes only a living art form when studied in its film context.

In this book I have made frequent use of Bergman's printed screenplays. Where no published version is available I have resorted to a film's "working script" (much more complete and less full of technical detail than an ordinary shooting script). But I have always kept the films in mind, and the purpose of the study is to analyze Ingmar Bergman, the writer of dialogue, and Ingmar Bergman, the creator of visual images. At best author and film-maker fuse, word and image become synchronized into a total vision. Then it becomes possible to follow Bergman's own advice —that the critic make "no distinction between writer and director in regard to film." [16]

After a biographical introduction and a chapter on Bergman's contribution as a playwright, the bulk of this study is devoted to the films of Ingmar Bergman, including those which he produced in collaboration with the novelist Ulla Isaksson (*Brink of Life* and *The Virgin Spring*) and a few based upon Bergman's revisions of literary works. On the whole, I have followed a chronological outline although, in some cases, a certain grouping of films has seemed justified in order to clarify common themes and similar points of view. However, the films treated out of chronological context are so few—most notably *Brink of Life*, *The Magician*, and *Persona*—that they should not prevent the student from being able to observe Bergman's growth and development as an artist.

BIRGITTA STEENE

Temple University

Contents

Chronology

1918 Born in the city of Uppsala, on July 14.
1937 Passed college entrance examination.
1938 Director at Mäster Olofsgården, Stockholm.
1941 Director at the Student Theater in Stockholm.
1942 *Death of Punch* (*Kaspers död*), first Bergman play to be produced.
1944 Director at the Hälsingborg City Theater.
      Torment (*Hets*), first film script.
1945 *Rachel and the Cinema Doorman* (*Rakel och biografvaktmästaren*), play produced at the Malmö City Theater.
1946 *Crisis* (*Kris*), first film directed by Bergman.
1947 Director at the Gothenburg City Theater.
      The Day Ends Early (*Dagen slutar tidigt*) and *To My Terror* (*Mig till skräck*) produced at the Gothenburg City Theater.
      Publication of *Jack Among the Actors* (*Jack hos skådespelarna*).
      The film *A Ship to India* (*Skepp till Indialand*).
1948 Publication of *Morality Plays* (*Moraliteter*).
      Torment produced as a play in Oslo and London (British title: *Frenzy*. Director: Peter Ustinov).
      The films *Port of Call* (*Hamnstad*) and *The Devil's Wanton* (*Fängelse*). The latter was first film written *and* directed by Bergman.
1949 The film *Three Strange Loves* (*Törst*).
1950 The film *To Joy* (*Till glädje*).
1951 The film *Illicit Interlude* (*Sommarlek*).
      The radio play *The City* (*Staden*).
1952 Director at the Malmö City Theater.
      Murder at Barjärna (*Mordet i Barjärna*) produced at the Malmö City Theater.
      The film *Secrets of Women* (*Kvinnors väntan*).

1953 The film *The Naked Night* (*Gycklarnas afton*).
1954 Publication of *Wood Painting* (*Trämålning*).
The film *A Lesson in Love* (*En lektion i kärlek*).
The ballet *Twilight Games* (*Skymningslekar*).
The Naked Night awarded a prize at a film festival in São Paulo, Brazil. Oddly enough, Bergman was first appreciated abroad in South America.
1955 *Wood Painting* produced at the Royal Dramatic Theater in Stockholm.
The films *Dreams* (*Kvinnodröm*) and *Smiles of a Summer Night* (*Sommarnattens leende*).
1956 International breakthrough. *Smiles of a Summer Night* awarded a prize at the Cannes film festival for its "poetic humor."
1957 The films *Wild Strawberries* (*Smultronstället*) and *The Seventh Seal* (*Det sjunde inseglet*).
The Seventh Seal awarded jury prize at the Cannes film festival.
1958 The films *Brink of Life* (*Nära livet*) and *The Magician* (*Ansiktet*).
Wild Strawberries awarded first prize at the Berlin film festival.
Brink of Life awarded director's prize at the Cannes film festival. (Actresses shared the prize for the best actress of the year.)
Joseph Bernstein Award for best foreign import (*The Seventh Seal*).
1959 Staged Stravinski's *The Rake's Progress* at the Royal Opera in Stockholm.
Staged Hjalmar Bergman's *Sagan* in Paris.
Staged *Faust* in London.
Married *Käbi Laretei*, Estonian-born pianist.
1960 The Films *The Virgin Spring* (*Jungfrukällan*) and *The Devil's Eye* (*Djävulens öga*).
The Virgin Spring awarded an Oscar as best foreign film of the year.
Publication of *Four Screenplays of Ingmar Bergman*.

1961   The film *Through a Glass Darkly* (*Såsom i en spegel*).
       American publication of *Wood Painting*.
       Staged Chekhov's *The Seagull* at the Royal Dramatic Theater in Stockholm.
1963   Head of the Royal Dramatic Theater in Stockholm.
       The films *Winter Light* (*Nattvardsgästerna*) and *The Silence* (*Tystnaden*).
       Publication of *En filmtrilogi* (Swedish edition of *Through a Glass Darkly, Winter Light,* and *The Silence*).
1964   The film *All These Women* (*För att inte tala om alla dessa kvinnor*).
1965   Bergman festival in Moscow.
       Awarded the Erasmus Prize in Amsterdam.
1966   Resigns as head of the Royal Dramatic Theater.
       The film *Persona*.
       Swedish publication of *Persona*, with an introductory essay on film-making.

CHAPTER 1

A Biographical Note

INGMAR BERGMAN is a playwright, theater director, and film-maker. Throughout his career he has remained faithful to both the stage and the screen, maintaining that "the theater is like a loyal wife, film is the big adventure, the expensive and demanding mistress—you worship both, each in its own way." [1]

Bergman's attraction to the stage and the screen seems to stem from an early age. He was only ten years old when he received his most memorable toy, a magic lantern and puppet theater, for which he made scenery and dolls, and wrote plays. When the couple in *The Devil's Wanton* relive their childhood, it is with the help of a similar apparatus. Bergman's love for the world of illusion was more than a child's fascination with playacting. Throughout his adolescence he used much of his pocket money to buy film for his *laterna magica* and film projector and he spent several nights a week at the cinema. He also attended the opera regularly but only seldom went to the theater. In 1935, however, he saw Olof Molander's epoch-making staging of Strindberg's *A Dream Play,* a production that was to leave a lasting impression on him. [2]

After passing his college entrance examination and doing his military service, Bergman began to study literature and art at the University of Stockholm. He wrote his literature thesis on Strindberg's *Keys to Heaven,* a composition that reads like a directorial stage copy, but he was more involved in amateur theater groups than in formal studies. He did not complete the work for his academic degree; nevertheless, his years at the University were invaluable, for they gave him an opportunity to try out his creative and directorial talents and also led to his first contacts with film producers.

Bergman made his debut in the theater as director of a Christian "settlement workshop," Mäster Olofsgården. Among his productions were Strindberg's *Lucky Per's Journey* and *Macbeth*, his favorite Shakespeare play. The chairman of the Student Theater in Stockholm, who saw the production of *Macbeth*, invited Bergman to talk about his work. Soon he was busy staging Strindberg's *The Pelican* for the Stockholm University theater group. He became known among the students as a director with a magic touch but also as a man of volatile temperament. One of the young actors in the workshop, Birger Malmsten (who later appeared in a number of Bergman's films, from *The Devil's Wanton* to *The Silence*), has recorded his early memories of Bergman: "His face always seemed to have an angry expression and he was considered to be very gifted but utterly crazy. He directed the play, holding a hammer in his hand, and he threw it from time to time at the young actors." [3]

By 1944 Bergman had left the University and now became a professional director at the City Theater in Hälsingborg, a city in the south of Sweden. The theater was on the verge of artistic and economic collapse, but in two years Bergman had transformed it into a very successful enterprise. He then moved on to the Gothenburg City Theater where his influence became equally strong. In 1952 he began a six-year directorship at the Malmö City Theater, one of the most modern playhouses in Europe, which during "the Bergman era" became known for its fine ensemble acting and well-balanced repertory, ranging from *Faust* to *The Merry Widow*. Many of the actors at the Malmö theater later became Bergman's favorite interpreters on the screen: Harriet Andersson, Bibi Andersson, Ingrid Thulin, and Max von Sydow.

Bergman's career in the theater culminated during the three years (1963–66) that he was head of Sweden's national stage, the Royal Dramatic Theater in Stockholm. All in all he has staged, between 1938 and 1966, some seventy-five productions, in addition to many television and radio plays. Among dramatists whose works he has produced we find Molière, Goethe, Ibsen, Strindberg, Chekhov, Pirandello, Brecht, Camus, Anouilh, Tennessee Williams, and Edward Albee.

Early in his career in the theater Bergman wrote plays for the stage (see next chapter). Relatively soon, however, he came to accept himself in the role of interpreter, which may have to do with the fact that for him "the theater represents . . . absolute objectivity." A stage director and a playwright are incompatible;

the latter's approach is subjective while the director must learn to
enter something more important than himself and become "a
member in a large body, a member of a collective group and sub-
ordinated to the demands of discipline and humbleness." [4]

When Bergman announced his resignation from the Royal Dramatic Theater early in 1966, one drama critic wrote:

It is difficult to hide a certain bitterness at Bergman's resignation. For
he has given the Royal Dramatic a shot of vitamins of a kind seldom
seen in its hundred and seventy-five years old history. . . . Ingmar
Bergman's brief leadership charged our theatrical life with new areas
of excitement. At last we got a creative temperament working with all
the resources of power in his hands, a Swedish Jean Vilar who was not
satisfied with directorial victories but wanted to transform our entire
view of the theater. . . . One has always sensed the vision that lay before him, with a national theater that deserved that name. If I am to be
honest, I would rather have done without some of his new films—no
matter how good they might be—in order to have seen that vision realized. [5]

Bergman will continue to work in the theater as a guest director, but it is clear that one of the reasons for his resignation from
the Royal Dramatic Theater was the fact that he wanted to devote more of his time to film-making. This is understandable since
his career in the cinema has been even more remarkable than his
contribution to the theater.

The Swedish film enjoyed its Golden Age in the early nineteen-
twenties. With the arrival of sound, Swedish directors felt that the
language problem prevented them from producing films for ex-
port. The lack of international competition may be one reason
why the nineteen-thirties became a period of artistic decline in
Swedish film-making, when trivial comedies and historical specta-
cles were produced with only the home market in mind. Finally,
in the early nineteen-forties, came the first signs of an attempt to
remedy the situation. Dr. Carl Anders Dymling, who was ap-
pointed managing director of Svensk Filmindustri, the leading
movie company in Sweden, tried to encourage younger talents.
Like Shakespeare who arrived in London at a time of fresh and
vital interest in the drama, Bergman came upon the scene at a
most opportune moment in the history of Swedish film-making.

Mrs. Stina Bergman, wife of the late playwright and novelist

Hjalmar Bergman, who had assumed the task of talent scout for Svensk Filmindustri, became interested in Ingmar Bergman (no kin) after reading an appreciative review of one of his early stage productions. Invited to the home of Mrs. Bergman, the young director appeared "shabby, ill-mannered and unshaven, with a derisive laughter that seemed to originate in the darkest corner of Inferno." But he also exuded "an unconcerned charm, which was so forceful that after a few hours' conversation I had to drink three cups of coffee in order to get back to normal." [6]

The result of the interview was that Bergman produced his first film script, *Torment (Hets)*, and was made the apprentice of Alf Sjöberg, who directed the film. With its cutting criticism of the autocratic Swedish school system, *Torment*—and its author—became a *cause célèbre*. A year later Bergman was allowed to direct his first picture, *Crisis (Kris)*. Since then he has directed one or two pictures a year. For most of them he has written the script. Making films has, says Bergman, "become a natural necessity, a need similar to hunger and thirst. For certain people to express themselves implies writing books, climbing mountains, beating children, or dancing the samba. I express myself by making films." [7]

Elsewhere Bergman has referred to film-making as "self-combustion and self-effusion." The creation of a film is an exacting work, "a tapeworm 2,500 meters long that sucks the life and spirit out of me. . . . When I am filming, I am ill." [8] No one can be unaware of Bergman's films as intensely personal statements, which, however, is not to say that they are highly private; it seems definitely a mistake to try to draw too close a parallel between his cinematic characters and actual people or to interpret his symbols only in terms of available biographical information.[9] Bergman's strength as an artist—apart from his unquestionable technical skill —lies in his ability to create characters who, although they are carriers of his personal ethics, have the abstract quality of people in a morality play, and to project these characters on a scene of great visual clarity and emotional intensity. Bergman is by no means a great and original thinker, but his themes and characters are banal in the sense that archetypes are banal, and in this lies their appeal to a large number of people. Siegfried Kracauer's theory of film-making, although dubious as a general thesis, certainly applies to Bergman: "What films reflect are not so much explicit credos as psychological dispositions—those deep layers of collective mentality which extend more or less below the dimension of consciousness." [10]

Turning from the immediate social reality around him, Bergman has focused his lens on an interior landscape, and much of his work emerges as an "allegory" on the progress of the soul—his own and, by inference, the soul of modern man. Citing O'Neill, Bergman has stated that any drama is worthless which does not deal with man's relationship to metaphysical questions. This artistic premise is no doubt connected with his personal background. As he once said to French film critic Jean Béranger: "To make films is to plunge to the very depth of childhood." [11]

Ernst Ingmar Bergman was born on July 14, 1918, the son of a Lutheran clergyman who later became court chaplain to the King of Sweden. Bergman's father often took his son on bicycle trips to the rural churches of Uppland, and while he preached the son would absorb the symbolic interior of the churches, their mural paintings and wood carvings, their popular renderings of biblical stories. Years later Bergman transformed some of these early memories into a play entitled *Wood Painting* (*Trämålning*), which eventually became the film *The Seventh Seal* (*Det sjunde inseglet*).

Bergman spent much of his childhood in the university town of Uppsala, staying with a widowed grandmother in a 14-room apartment, which was arranged then as it had been in 1890 when the grandmother moved in there as a bride. Bergman's other companion was an old servant, full of fairy tales and country stories. He experienced a great sense of security at his grandmother's place and later on in life when he wanted to describe a sense of completeness, he could do so by referring to this part of his childhood: "I know where I am, how I stand, who I am. . . . This feeling is identical to the sense of security, of seeing clearly and being sure that my vision of life was correct, that I had back there when I was a boy living with my grandmother in Uppsala." [12]

Bergman's tendency to bypass social problems—even in his earliest films society is abstracted to represent the destructiveness and evil of the adult world as opposed to the innocence of youth —for metaphysical questions probably received a new impetus during the nineteen-forties. Bergman's formative years as an artist coincided with the emergence of a new generation of Swedish writers whose mood was one of existential *Angst* and religious skepticism. The encounter with this "school of the forties" may have helped crystallize Bergman's own doubts about God although his pessimism was never as complete as that of the literary group. The Kafka fever that raged in Sweden about the same time may also have shaped Bergman's concept of a distant and silent God, of God as a need but not as fulfillment, and of modern man's rootlessness in a world of outmoded values. Yet, the brooding over questions of guilt and reconciliation, punishment and forgiveness that permeates both Kafka's and Bergman's work has its common denominator in the Protestantism and worship of the Father as a distant Power under which both artists grew up. To both of them the home offered protection, but also paralysis and isolation.[13]

Bergman has always admitted that he is deeply rooted in Swedish art and life. He belongs in fact to a category of artists that might be disappearing in the Western world: artists for whom the personal vision fuses with a feeling of national identity. Bergman needs his Swedish tradition and milieu, not only for inspiration but for a sense of security, without which he admits he could not work. He has often referred to the feeling of panic that can grasp him in a totally foreign surrounding, and he has never accepted offers to make films abroad although the financial benefits would probably be considerable. Typical is a passage from his brief essay, "A Page from My Diary," which describes a day during the shooting of *The Virgin Spring*, with everyone being somewhat downcast until two cranes appeared overhead and everyone dropped his work to watch. The company went back to work happy and enchanted by the experience and Bergman mentions his feelings of relief and security in this "Swedish" atmosphere and among these people; he decides at this time to reject an American film offer.[14]

CHAPTER 2

Ingmar Bergman as a Playwright

PERHAPS the most interesting aspect of Bergman's early contact with the theater is the fact that his work with amateur
groups stimulated him to write his first plays for the stage. In the
summer of 1942 he completed in quick succession a number of
short dramas: *Death of Punch* (*Kaspers död*), *Travel Companions* (*Reskamrater*), *The Station* (*Stationen*), *The Lonely Ones*
(*De ensamma*), *The Fun Fair* (*Tivolit*), *The Full Moon* (*Full-
månen*), *The Fog* (*Dimman*), *About a Murderer* (*Om en mör-
dare*). Of these only *The Fun Fair* and *Death of Punch* were ever
performed, and only the latter exists in manuscript form.

I Death of Punch (Kaspers död)

The plot: Death of Punch revolves around Kasper (the Swedish name for Punch), who leaves his wife to dance and drink with
prostitutes and criminals. But suddenly during his gay escapades
Kasper dies. The climax of the play consists of a long speech by
the title character as he sits on his grave waiting to meet God.—

In its metaphysical approach *Death of Punch* adheres to a line
in modern Swedish drama which began with Strindberg's post-
Inferno production[1] and was revived in 1918 by the young Pär
Lagerkvist in a series of one-act plays called *Den svåra stunden*
(*The Difficult Hour*). The title of Lagerkvist's dramas alludes to
the moment of death when man is still clinging to life, contem-
plating the absurdity of living and waiting in the dark for God to
answer his prayers. Lagerkvist's desperate, expressionistic cry for
a meaning in life reverberates in all of Bergman's plays. A program notice to one of his early productions for the stage—Olle
Hedberg's *Rabies*—indicates that he was well acquainted with
Lagerkvist's metaphysical point of view. Hedberg, says Bergman,
did not even have "the belief in Pär Lagerkvist's blind and dead
god who sits frozen in ice in his heaven."[2] The image of a god

25

"frozen in ice," which suggests a satanic rather than divine context, has reference also to Bergman's own works, where the philosophical core is often man's ambivalent experiencing of God as both a diabolic and a beatific power.

Death of Punch also shares with Lagerkvist's plays a tone that borders on the hysterical. For both playwrights the emotional excessiveness is a substitute for dramatic action. Their plays are conceived as loud protests but lack tension and conflict between the characters. The real weakness of Bergman's drama lies, however, in its ending: the author dares not pursue Kasper's pessimistic point of view but performs a philosophical somersault. God's presence is suddenly proclaimed by a figure who plays the role of a kind judge. This incredible *deus ex machina* attaches a happy end to a play, the very tone of which denies the existence of transcendental powers.

II Jack Among the Actors (Jack bland skådespelarna)

Originally written for the radio in 1946, Bergman's next play avoids such easy solutions and shows a firmer grasp of the dramatic medium.

The plot: A corporal, Jack Kasparsson, joins a provincial theater group led by a director he has never met. The action develops along the lines of a Pirandelloan dissolution of identities: three actors—a husband, wife, and lover—perform a triangle drama of soap opera quality and become the parts they play. When the husband dies, Jack Kasparsson steps in as the lover, while the former lover shoulders the mantle of married cuckold. The play—and life—can go on as before, until the director, still invisible, decides to dissolve the troupe. In the end, the director appears before Jack and reveals his true nature.—

Spleen and fatalism permeate most of Bergman's youthful works. Human beings are conceived as marionettes shuffled around by a deterministic potentate. It is a view frequently expressed in the works of an earlier generation of Swedish writers, to whom Bergman has acknowledged his indebtedness.[3] The Director in *Jack Among the Actors* echoes many characters in the novels and plays of Hjalmar Söderberg (1869–1941) and Hjalmar Bergman (1883–1931) as he tells Jack Kasparsson: "And I have sat there and pulled the strings. Jerked and pulled, and the people have obeyed me. They hopped and danced and whirled and

I was amused. . . . I mastered many and was their God and their Devil."

The Director is Bergman's first clear conception of the paradoxical monster-God, who will later emerge as "the spider god" in the films *Through A Glass Darkly* and *Winter Light*. But the need for a loving Father-God exists in man. As the Director leaves the stage and the curtain falls, Jack Kasparsson cries out to this God: "Is there no one who can help me? Dear God, help me. Yes, dear God in heaven, help me, God, you who are somewhere, who must be somewhere, you must help me. Don't you see that I am little and afraid and that it is so damned dark."

III   Rachel and the Cinema Doorman
(Rachel och biografvaktmästaren)

The juxtaposition of metaphysical probing and a psychological as well as archetypal (the Judge, the Director) conception of character is maintained by Bergman in the three dramas that he published in 1948 under the joint title of *Morality Plays* (*Moraliteter*). Bergman's implied definition of the genre aims at a play which is a moral fable but not a fully worked-out religious allegory. Nor do his plays have the simple tension between good and evil, obedience and temptation that is characteristic of their medieval prototype. Bergman's "morality play" is a modern drama in which complicated situations and attitudes often can be unraveled in terms of profane psychology. This is especially true of the first play in the collection: *Rachel and the Cinema Doorman*.

The plot: A scholar, Eugen Lobelius, and his wife Rachel are expecting weekend guests, Kaj and Mia Hesster, to their summer house in the Stockholm archipelago. While Eugen is in town on an errand, Kaj arrives alone and ahead of schedule; his pregnant wife will come later. Kaj appears the very opposite of Eugen: sensuous and bohemian while Eugen is impotent and pedantic. An attempt by Kaj to seduce Rachel fails but releases the tension in her marriage. Eugen returns; there is an argument and he insists upon a divorce, then disappears into the garden with a gun. Now Mia enters upon the scene and reveals Kaj's childlike dependence upon her. In the last scene Eugen comes back, and Petra, the old housekeeper, tries coaxingly to take the gun away from him. In the skirmish Mia is shot accidentally and killed on the spot.—

While Bergman's earliest plays are interesting parallels to his
first cinematic attempts with their emphasis on adolescent despair
and a deterministic view of life, *Rachel and the Cinema Doorman*
suggests a somewhat later phase in Bergman's production when
the point of view is female and Woman, rather than God, is man's
support in life. Mia's senseless death is analogous to the calami-
tous end that meets many women in Bergman's films, but it also
anticipates their frequent role of sacrificial victims. In dying, Mia
releases Kaj from his evil intentions and brings him to a state of
tranquility. Watching his wife's dead body, Kaj whispers: "I stand
inside the darkness in my little black cube and believe that it is
sailing through a pitch-dark nothingness, and I am quite calm and
almost happy."

Rachel and the Cinema Doorman was used as the basis for one
of the stories in Bergman's episodic film *Secrets of Women*. In his
film version, Bergman omitted Mia's character, no doubt because
he left out the metaphysical pattern altogether and reduced the
drama to a psychological triangle. In the film it is Rachel who
takes over the role of healer: Eugen needs a mother and Rachel
finally accepts a maternal rather than sexual relationship with her
husband. Also, in the original play Eugen is depicted as a pam-
pered child, but the mother figure is played by the old housekeeper, and Rachel's changing attitude toward her husband is no
more than suggested.

In the stage version, Rachel is conceived as a frustrated woman
but also as a "soul" led into temptation by Kaj, "the cinema doorman." The housekeeper, a kind of chorus figure with a salvation-
ist's need to see human life in terms of religious archetypes, relegates Kaj to Satan's cohort:

. . . sometimes a person comes along, a person you don't want to
shake hands with or speak to, one of the devil's crowd. *He* has sent
them out to collect souls for Hell. . . . They can talk and laugh and
move like other people. But if you have a sensitive nose, you notice that
they smell funny. . . . That fellow out there has that strange smell. I
am sixty-five. I know that he can do any amount of evil. It is his mission. I have seen that before. And it is horrible and you want to run
and hide but you can't do it, for they follow you.

Although Rachel is the central character in the play, it is Kaj
who interests Bergman most. He might be called Jack Kaspars-

son's successor, for he has begun where Jack left off, crying to
heaven for help against his fear of being alone: "What was I to
do? I stood there in the dark, and fear sat straddle-legged across
my back. Then I began to cry for help. And since I had no one in
particular to turn to, I turned to God."

But the god (never capitalized) who answers Kaj is a manipu-
lating power, a kin to the Director in *Jack Among the Actors:* "Do
you know what god did? (Pause) Well, he took me as I was with
my evil and fear and darkness and all that, and threw me into one
circumstance after another. And he forced me to use my evil and
my fear and my darkness. I had done many people wrong before.
But now I was forced, with wide-open eyes, to torture and torment to the right and left." From this monster-god only Mia (Maria) or Charity can save Kaj.

IV The Day Ends Early (Dagen slutar tidigt)

In the second play in the collection, *The Day Ends Early*, Bergman returns to the partly supernatural plot of *Death of Punch*.

The plot: An old lady, Mrs. Åström, has heard a voice ordering
her to tell five people that they shall die the following day. She is
to accompany them on their journey "to relieve their anxiety." The
main part of the action revolves around one of those destined to
die, Jenny Sjuberg, a business woman. In the evening she gathers
with some friends for a midsummer night's party. Following the
suggestion of her business partner and former husband, Robert
van Hijn, whose name has diabolic connotations,[4] Jenny observes
some of her guests from a hideout in the garden. This kaleido-
scopic view of human life culminates with a scene in which Finger-
Pella, a homosexual beauty operator who is also among those
picked out to die, reveals his frantic fear. To soothe her own panic
Jenny seduces her younger sister's lover, Ole, but is unmasked as a
desperate and aging woman. Later she approaches Peter, an actor
who has entertained the group with a puppet theater performance
of *Everyman* (one more example of the frequent play-within-the-
play approach in Bergman's work). Suddenly Jenny is called to a
mental hospital to verify the identity of Mrs. Åström, who turns
out to be an old alcoholic brought back to the institution after an
escape. In the waiting room Jenny meets all the other victims of
Mrs. Åström's hallucination, with the exception of Finger-Pella.
Just as they have accepted a rational explanation of the whole

episode, they learn that Mrs. Åström has suddenly been taken
ill with pneumonia. At the same time Oscar, Finger-Pella's friend,
reports to Jenny that his lover has been killed by a streetcar. In
the last scene of the play Mrs. Åström appears with the five victims; they are all dead and find themselves in a great void. Jenny
cries out in a prayer that echoes Kasper's and Jack's final speeches:
"I believe we are all very scared. Someone said you should pray
when you feel such fear. Even if you don't believe in anything.
. . . Dear God! You who are in the darkness and the wind, help
me because I am an unimportant and scared human being who
doesn't see anything and doesn't understand and doesn't believe."—

The Day Ends Early has been called "an overly compressed tale
with a contemporary motif." [5] It brings to mind Pär Lagerkvist's
collection of stories entitled *Onda sagor* (*Evil Tales*) as well as
the aforementioned group of expressionistic dramas, *The Difficult
Hour.* As in Lagerkvist, the use of the supernatural throws the
human condition into a much sharper relief than would an ordinary realistic play. Jenny Sjuberg's erotic escapades may be the
result of the sexual hunger of an aging woman; but they are also a
desperate human attempt to find some meaning in life before it is
too late. Finger-Pella's homosexuality is not merely a social aberration but a symbol of man's loneliness in the face of death.

Yet, *The Day Ends Early* is more ambitious than successful. Instead of the fusion of psychological motivation and archetypal
pattern that characterized *Rachel and the Cinema Doorman, The
Day Ends Early* is a dramatic hybrid, part mental thriller, part
supernatural vision; the drama never becomes an integrated
whole, and it lacks the ambiguity of the earlier play. From the
point of view of characterization, the epilogue—the meeting of
the dead—is awkward since we know next to nothing about any
of the deceased except Mrs. Sjuberg. In all likelihood Bergman
intended Mrs. Sjuberg's experiences to form an illustration of the
despair sensed by all in the final scene. But such a conception
demands a far more stylized form than Bergman has given his
play.

V   To My Terror (Mig till skräck)

The last play in the collection, *To My Terror,* is among other
things an ironic commentary upon the other two.

The plot: The central character is Paul, a writer of metaphysical novels, whose publisher tells him: "To talk about God is not always artistic." Paul has pursued his religious point of view with little variation and, according to his editor, he is about "to hang himself in his own spaghetti." During a talk with his wife, it transpires that Paul is willing to compromise with the publisher about the religious ending of his latest book. As it turns out, he does not have to make any changes, but in principle he has denied himself as an artist. The rest of his life is a pathetic failure and a series of little lies which infect his marriage as well as his relationship with all people. Isak, an old Jew who is a friend of Paul's grandmother, explains why Paul's denial of his artistic integrity was unforgivable: "You went into nothingness with open eyes. Others don't see it. But you chose it in clear consciousness and in full possession of your senses."—

Philosophically, *To My Terror* marks a new phase in Bergman's development: the beginning of his existentialist approach to life and the end of his deterministic *Weltanschauung*. But from a dramatic point of view it is the least successful of the *Morality Plays*. In three acts Bergman telescopes twenty years of Paul's life. The long time lapse merely accentuates the weakness in Bergman's conception of Paul: he is a static character whose mind is made up early in the play and who experiences no inner conflict, only a prolonged sense of degradation. The drama has a strong quality of self-accusation with the result that Paul emerges as a rather disagreeable person; the repeated testimonies of sympathy for him, given by the other characters, sound merely false.

To My Terror is the most explanatory of Bergman's plays. To make up for its quality of discussion drama, Bergman inserts two comic figures, Grandmother and her housekeeper Mean. They are colorful, amusing, and a little mysterious in their roles of evil fairy and good fairy: Mean controls the situation in the first act and protects Paul and his young fiancée as they arrive at Grandmother's place. In the second act Paul and Kersti have fallen under the spell of Grandmother, an unfeeling hag of a woman (and an early study of Isak Borg's mother in *Wild Strawberries*), whose presence breathes unhappiness and destruction. Both Mean and Grandmother are mythic figures who "never die," projections of good and evil forces in Paul; once Paul has lost his integrity, Grandmother comes out of hiding, and in the scene where Paul's and Kersti's marriage collapses, Grandmother hovers around the couple like an ill omen. But Grandmother and Mean never clash; the one merely succeeds the other—a further sign of the basically undramatic structure of the play.

VI The City (Staden)

The embryo of Bergman's next play, *The City*, which was written for the radio in 1951, can be found in *To My Terror*, in a scene where Paul reads from a book of his youth:

Then Joakim said: It is strange to think that the earth shall be Hell . . . that all human life is a failure, all striving in vain, all desire is indifference, all joy a relief of sorrow and pain. We must be crushed and ravaged and our self-sufficiency wiped out, for it is of the devil. Then that moment will come when we can choose between God and annihilation.

In *Morality Plays* Bergman tested the religious alternative. In *The City*, whose central character is an unsuccessful artist by the name of Joakim Naken, only loneliness and the prospect of annihilation remain. When *The City* was rebroadcast in 1966, Bergman told his listeners in a radio interview that his play was written after a crisis in his life: he had been "kicked out" from Svensk Filmindustri; he had left the Gothenburg City Theater where he had been a director; his affiliation with the Intimate Theater in Stockholm as a consultant had been unhappy; his private life was deeply disharmonic. When he finally began to work his way out of the depression, he felt a need to transform his experiences into a play.

The plot: Joakim Naken has returned to the city of the past ("the city of the ruins of memory"). It is summer; the air is hot and suffocating. During his walk through the streets he meets a pastor who believes life should be regarded as a correctional institution; he runs into a former mistress who has experienced a painful divorce; and in a major scene he is confronted with his wife, who has been condemned to death for having killed three of her children. Surrealistic characters also appear: Oliver Mortis, "the death in your spirit," accompanies Joakim to his wife; an old worker called "the Pump" tells Joakim of strange events that once anticipated a disastrous period in the history of the

city. Now "the Pump" has again observed odd aberrations in
nature. The city is in danger.

Suddenly the scene changes from summer to winter. Joakim is
now on his way to his grandmother's house. He meets a poet
whom he advises to follow the literary vogue and not be too pro-
ductive. Arriving at his grandmother's he runs into all the people
he has seen earlier. His first encounter with them was only an
evil dream. Yet, the city will be destroyed. But in the same moment, Joakim discovers that, in spite of his spiritual bankruptcy,
he has in him the foundation of a new city. It is his grandmother
who gives him hope by telling him he must believe in "a sense of
fellowship, in the keen expectations of tomorrow, in . . . your
own possibilities."—

In spite of its dark, nihilistic tone, *The City* would seem to end
on a less pessimistic note than the earlier plays with their cry for a
God in the dark. But the last part of the drama is not convincing.
Joakim's optimism is intellectualized; his cathartic return to his
grandmother's house is little more than a piece of childhood nostalgia. Grandmother's pedagogical advice may be a moral booster
to Joakim, but it is unmotivated in the dramatic context. We are
not made to understand why Joakim should listen more to her
voice than to the destructive ones he has encountered throughout
the major part of the play.

The name of Bergman's alter ego, Joakim Naken, suggests an
unmasked and defenseless person (naken = naked) and also
brings to mind a speech in *The Day Ends Early* when Jenny Sjuberg tells Peter, the actor: "Now I have stripped to the skin [liter-
ally translated: undressed myself naked] before you, Mr. Peter,
and the same thing happened to me as to a person I saw in a film.
When he undressed and unwound the bandages around his face
and hands, there was neither body nor face nor hands. There was
nothing."

In his nihilistic but vulnerable position Joakim Naken is also
reminiscent of the central character in Strindberg's *To Damascus;*
like the Stranger in Strindberg's drama, Joakim Naken finds himself at point zero when the play begins: "I have buried myself in
women, in religious ecstacy, and in my faith in a so-called artistic
activity, but all has been in vain. The tension has only increased,
and now I give it all up and wait for the executors."

The rest of the drama is clearly patterned upon Strindberg's play: it is a station drama in which the action is composed of a series of stops or encounters with important people in the protagonist's life. The confessional yet accusing tone of Joakim Naken's speech has the same ambivalence as that of the penitential but stubborn Stranger, and the ending of *The City*, with its attempted reconciliation to life, has the abstract quality of Strindberg's cry for "resignation and humility" in *To Damascus*.

Joakim Naken's emotional extremism with regard to women, his oscillation between violent hatred and nostalgic love, bears a resemblance not only to *To Damascus* but to all of Strindberg's marriage dramas. In listening to Joakim's venomous outbursts before his wife in prison, one seems to hear an echo from *The Father* or *The Dance of Death*:

If hell existed, I would wish you there. I could kill you for what you've done to me! You make me sick and I shall never stop hating you, and I shall slander your memory so that your glory of martyrdom is taken away from you and your wings are torn from your shoulders! You who were a single curse, a nightmare, a poisoning! Ugh! May your death be as meaningless as your life has been!

Likewise, Joakim's summary view of the relationship between man and woman is a synopsis of Strindbergian love-hatred:

Isn't it strange! In the midst of a war of life and death, the parties hold their breath and regard each other kindly, almost with sympathy. They seek consolation in each other and sleep side by side, until, suddenly, one of them fires up, driven by some shameful memory, and assaults the other. And then the war is in full swing. The intervals are called happiness, the exhaustion reconciliation.

Bergman has freely admitted his dependence upon Strindberg, whom he discovered at an early age and absorbed with all the receptiveness of a young adolescent: "I began to read Strindberg when I was ten. It was a shattering and fundamental experience. His very dialogue burnt into my flesh. Later when I began to write, I was of course dependent upon this, and only slowly, very slowly, could I create a dialogue of my own." [6] In *The City* the very speech patterns and the rhythm of the language seem imbued with Strindberg's spirit. One might note, however, a strong affinity in temperament between Strindberg and Ingmar Bergman. The older playwright lent his voice to the younger, but their experiencing of life was fundamentally the same: a strong rebellion against parental authority, including that of God, the Father; an ambivalent attitude toward women, switching from worship to disillusionment and hatred; an excessive sensitivity to sound and smell; a tendency to regard dreams and nightmares as more real than daily activities. Bergman has often mentioned the difficulties he had as a child in separating the realities of day and night, of wakefulness and sleep. Thus his dream-play technique in *The City*—the fluid form with its rapid changes in climate and scenery and the dreamlike conception of the secondary characters—is not merely a Strindbergian reconstruction but would seem to grow out of Bergman's own private experiencing of life.

Bergman has often had a need to reject his early work in the theater and the cinema, possibly in an affort to disarm the critics. That he agreed to a rebroadcast of *The City* seems, however, to refute an earlier statement in which he said: "I regard my early plays as dead, passé, gone. I have forbidden any further production of them." [7]

VII   Wood Painting (Trämålning)

On the same occasion Bergman claimed that *Wood Painting*, his last play to date, marked his actual dramatic debut, while his previous works for the stage were "only immature preliminary exercises." *Wood Painting* was written in 1954 as a dramatic exercise for Bergman's students at the Malmö City Theater. The play is a minor pedagogical masterpiece with eight characters who all have approximately equal time on the stage. The work might best be described as a study in a series of attitudes toward death. Bergman calls it a morality play. Like several of Bergman's earlier dramas, *Wood Painting* takes place in a borderland between life and death.

The plot: Jöns, the Squire, is on his way home from the Holy Land with his master, the Knight. They have reached the shores of Sweden, a country just ravaged by the plague. During the night they meet a witch who has been burnt at the stake; they run into a smith chasing his unfaithful wife, who has disappeared with an actor ("a lover without love"); they see the Virgin Mary with her child, and they are greeted by the Knight's virtuous wife. In the end the plague claims them all, except the Virgin and her baby, and they dance away across the dark hills.—

Although *Wood Painting* is no more than a dramatic sketch, based on a *Totentanz* motif, it contains the major themes of Bergman's entire production: the shortcomings of love, and man's fear of the void inside and outside himself, which is also related to his attitude toward God. The first theme is illustrated by the infidelity of the smith's wife and the irrational behavior of her husband: one moment he is ready to murder her; the next he falls down to worship her. The Squire provides a commenting voice: "Love is the blackest of all plagues. . . . Love is contagious as the flu, it steals your blood, your strength, your independence, your morals if you have any. Love is a taxing grimace that ends in a yawn."

The Squire is a materialist who can only fill his spiritual void with cynical irony: "This is my gospel. My little stomach is my globe, my head is my eternity and my hands are two wonderful suns. My legs are the lost pendulums of time and my dirty feet are two splendid starting points for my philosophy. My world is a Jöns-world . . . believable to no one but me, ridiculous to all, also to myself, meaningless before heaven and indifferent to hell."

The Knight, on the other hand, is a restless seeker of God who cannot accept a life without spiritual guidance but whose experiencing of the divine is full of uncertainty:

Each morning and evening I stretch my arms toward the Saints, toward God. . . . Again and again I am shaken with absolute certainty. Through the mists of spiritual listlessness God's nearness strikes me, like the strokes of a huge bell. Suddenly my emptiness is filled with music, almost without key but as if carried by innumerable voices. Then I cry through all my darkness, and my cry is like a whisper: "To your glory, O God! To your glory I live! To your glory! So I cry in the dark. Then the dreadful thing happens. The certainty dies as if someone had blown it out. The huge bell is silent, darkness pulsates even blacker, it pushes against my neck and belches out through my mouth.

The Squire and the Knight form the intellectual poles in Bergman's metaphysics. The other characters in *Wood Painting* approach death and the idea of an afterlife in a primitive or intuitive way. Maria's voice is a hymn to the divinity. The Knight's wife faces the end with a kind of matter-of-factness that does not ask any questions nor makes any protests. The young witch has formed a pact with the devil and has died in ecstasy. The actor belongs to a breed of men who consider themselves so unique that

they cannot believe in their own annihilation. When death sur-
prises him, he reacts like the smith and his wife who are filled
with a strong, elemental fear.

Although *Wood Painting* is interesting as a depository for Bergman's metaphysics, it reveals more plainly than his earlier dramas
his weaknesses as a playwright: a schematic conception of character and a verbose and overly rhetorical language. These artistic
flaws are also present in many of Bergman's films, but gradually
he has come to substitute image and camera movement for the
superficial psychology and flowery yet often abstract dialogue
that at times encumbers his works for the stage.

CHAPTER 3

Early Films: The Adolescent Point of View

I Torment (Hets)

INGMAR BERGMAN'S first produced screenplay was *Torment:* the film was directed by Alf Sjöberg and was released in 1944.

The plot: Torment takes place in a boys' school in Stockholm; in the conservative home of one of the pupils, Jan-Erik Widgren; and in the cheap lodging of a young girl from a tobacconist's shop. Jan-Erik finds the girl (Berta) drunk in the street. He takes her to her apartment and learns that she fears the visit of a strange man. Later we get to know that this man is Caligula, Jan-Erik's sadistic Latin teacher.

The story reaches its climax when Jan-Erik one day finds Berta dead in her bed. In the hall sits Caligula, shaking with fear. He is taken to the police station but is later released: an autopsy shows that Berta has died from a heart condition. Caligula now reports Jan-Erik to the principal and the boy is expelled from school. When the film ends, Jan-Erik is in Berta's empty apartment. He is visited by the principal who offers him his support. The final shots juxtapose Caligula, crouching on the steps outside Berta's apartment, fearing the consequences of his malevolence, and Jan-Erik, who steps out in the sunshine, feeling victorious since he has overcome his dread of authority as represented by Caligula.—

Jan-Erik is no angry young man. That role is played by his schoolmate Sandman, a disciple of Nietzsche and an echo of Strindberg the misogynist. Jan-Erik, on the other hand, is a dreamer; he seeks Berta's company because he is a young romantic in need of affection, and not because of any conscious effort to rebel or break out of his social class. But with his attachment to the girl follows a growing awareness that his own milieu is founded on untenable precepts. At the end of the film Jan-Erik knows that his school and home environment is wrong in its autocratic way of life. Yet, he does not try to destroy it; he merely leaves it behind.

Torment is an apolitical film, depicting a young man's maturing process in a world of patriarchal authority; therefore, it seems unfortunate that Alf Sjöberg, in directing the film, added some references to Nazism: Caligula (a Himmler type) reads the Swedish Nazi newspaper *Dagsposten*. This is an irrelevant allusion since Bergman wants to emphasize Caligula's role of abstract force: ". . . there are many kinds of Caligulas, large and small, rather innocuous ones and repulsive monsters, obvious or insidious. But a Caligula can always be recognized by one thing: he creates hatred, staleness, destruction among people." [1]

Caligula's role is the most dramatic one in the film, oscillating between the normal and the insane. Such ambivalence is reflected in Bergman's attitude toward his character: on the one hand Caligula is treated as a responsible person and condemned on moral grounds; on the other, he is presented as an unfortunate victim of a mental disorder, a sick man in need of understanding. But the actor (Stig Järrel) who created the part on the screen failed to convey any feelings that might arouse our pity, possibly because he carried his interpretation to the point of caricature.

The three worlds that touch upon each other in *Torment* are all literary clichés: the school as tyranny; the family as a prison; Berta, the fallen woman, as initiation into adulthood. What saves Bergman's story from banality is the way in which he makes each world throw light upon the others. Jan-Erik and Caligula are enemies, but it is Berta who unknowingly brings them into open warfare, and it is in her world that their roles become reversed: Caligula is unmasked and Jan-Erik emerges as the victor. Berta herself is no Mary of the gutter but is as much a victim of the world that Caligula represents as is Jan-Erik. She, too, is young and helpless before the experienced malice of adults.

Jan-Erik's home is merely another version of the same pattern, although in a more subdued, "civilized" form. In a revealing dinner scene, the father is shown presiding at one end of the huge table; his wife's attitude toward him is submissive and apologetic. The father is the Caligula of the home, the mother an older image of tyrannized Berta. Jan-Erik is caught between the two, receiving love from his mother, reprimands and angry lectures from his father.

The tension between adulthood and youth, austere discipline and *Sturm und Drang*, that permeates *Torment* has its counterpart in the style in which the film is produced. It has been argued that Alf Sjöberg imposed a controlled cinematic form upon the uncontrolled frenzy of Bergman's script.[2] But it seems more correct to see Sjöberg's technique, which moves between studied estheticism and expressionistic, exaggerated images—the influence from the American thriller is also evident—as an effort on his part to follow the moods of the script writer: to transmit the coldness and lack of rapport between milieu and character which is an important element in *Torment*, but also to convey the subjective fury in which the entire script is conceived.

II A Ship to India (Skepp till Indialand)

Two other scripts by Ingmar Bergman were filmed during the nineteen-forties: *Woman Without a Face* (*Kvinna utan ansikte*) and *Eva*, both of them directed by Gustaf Molander. All the films that Bergman himself made during the same period were based on the works of other writers. In some cases he and Herbert Grevenius, a playwright in the quiet, realistic vein, collaborated on an adaptation.

The most interesting of these films are *Crisis* (*Kris*), *It Rains Upon Our Love* (*Det regnar på vår kärlek*), *A Ship to India* (*Skepp till Indialand*), and *Port of Call* (*Hamnstad*). It will be sufficient to review briefly two of these. I have chosen *A Ship to India* and *Port of Call* because they demonstrate best Bergman's technical versatility. In common with all of his films from this time they have an adolescent point of view. The adult world is, with a few exceptions, cruel, hypocritical or at best indifferent. The young people are, like Jan-Erik and Berta in *Torment*, victims and helpless dreamers. They offer a kind of passive resistance against parental and social authority; yet they often give the impression of being drifters and escapists, standing outside the larger, conventional community. Jacques Siclier has pointed out the affinity of the young persons in Bergman's early films to the literary romantic hero of a century ago, whose rebellion was a form of rejection of reality: "If he [Bergman] has made his own a certain adolescent revolt, it is less in order to defy a precise social condition than to express a certain difficulty in existing, a certain dissatisfaction with life [*mal de vivre*] of which one can find the origin in the romanticism of the xixth century." [3]

The important thing for Bergman's lonely individual is to form a bond with another human being. The strength to survive lies in togetherness. "One cannot just be alone," says Sally, the young girl in *A Ship to India*. "One must have someone to care for. One must have someone to love. Else one might as well be dead."

The plot: A Ship to India deals with four people, each of whom has a dream. Alexander Blom, a captain and father, dreams of leaving his small salvage boat for a big ship to "Indialand"; his wornout wife Alice longs for a small cottage in the country; their hunchback son Johannes wants to break away from the parental bondage; Sally, a nightclub girl, would like to be taken care of by a kind man whom she could love. These four dreams cross each other and, in part, destroy each other.

When the film begins, Johannes has just returned home after seven years at sea. He looks up his first love, Sally, who no longer wants him. Except for the very end, the rest of the film is a single flashback, during which we learn that it was Johannes' father who brought Sally home, with the intention of fleeing with her to "Indialand." But Johannes falls in love with Sally, who, like a great many of Bergman's women, plays the role of a catalyst: she can cure Johannes of his disability which is psychological—the outward sign of parental neglect. But Alexander Blom forces his son to work as a diver; then, in a fit of jealousy, he tries to murder him. Johannes is saved but his father flees to his room, where he destroys a collection of ships and exotic objects. Finally, he attempts to commit suicide but fails.—

The important relationship in *A Ship to India* is that of the young couple, Johannes and Sally. The parental world is vicious and destructive; the mother, too, is possessive rather than loving. As in the case of Caligula in *Torment*, there is a suggestion that evil stems from our frustrated hopes and dreams: the desperation of the father is the result of his lack of contact with others.

A Ship to India ends on a note of conciliation as Johannes tries again to convince Sally to go with him. There is no love between them. In a review of the film, Erik Ulrichsen has referred to their relationship as a form of mutual mental hygiene. [4] Sally has cured Johannes; perhaps he will be able to help her out of her loneliness.

This optimistic note at the end is what separates A Ship to India from its cinematic source: the Carné and Duvivier films of the nineteen-thirties. Like his predecessors, Bergman conveys a deterministic point of view but his young couples are never as completely doomed as the characters in the French films.

It is in scene-painting and lighting that Carné's and Duvivier's spirit emerges most clearly in A Ship to India. Night pictures abound, the atmosphere is misty and poetic, the camera emphasizes the gloomy detail. Such lyrical realism forms the essence of all of Bergman's early films except Port of Call, in which the romantic night mood is gone.

III   Port of Call (Hamnstad)

The setting of Port of Call is the harbor slum of Gothenburg, and the camera is almost documentary in its faithful depiction of the port and the factory where the main character, Berit, works. It is a technique reminiscent of nonfictional British films, but an interview with Bergman in a Gothenburg newspaper at the time of the shooting of Port of Call reveals that he was working under the influence of the Italian neo-realistic school. Bergman mentions in particular Rossellini's Open City in which he had detected "the melody of postwar thought." [5]

The plot: The story, freely adapted by Bergman from a synopsis by Olle Länsberg, tells of a sailor, Gösta, who returns home after eight years at sea. On the pier one night he passes a group of people who are watching the arrival of an ambulance: a girl has jumped into the water and is taken to the hospital. Later Gösta meets the girl (Berit) in a dance hall and they spend the night together. It is a casual relationship and no bonds are formed between the two.

In a few flashbacks we learn that Berit is the product of a split home. She has tried to escape her religious, pedantic mother by moving in with a young man but has subsequently been sent to a correctional institution. When Gösta meets her, she is under the surveillance of a guardian, Mr. Vilander. Because Vilander previously has had unfortunate experiences when girls like Berit were to be trusted, he is now ready to send her back to an institution at the slightest suspicion. Haunted, Berit meets Gösta again and the two decide to stow away on a ship. But at the last moment they change their minds and stay.—

Bergman's simple credo in *A Ship to India* that "Love conquers all" is made even more explicit in *Port of Call*. The couple is again the important entity; togetherness gives strength and fighting spirit. "We won't give up," says Gösta at the end. Yet, nothing in his character or in the social situation indicates that he or Berit will be able to break the vicious circle in which Berit is caught. The problem is not really personal, and the initiative and help must come from the outside. Gösta as a type is incapable of handling Berit's problem: in the most impressive scene in the film— an expressionistic rendering of Gösta's pangs of conscience—he emerges as a modern romantic full of existentialist *Angst*, and hardly as the pillar of strength that the situation demands.

In handling Berit's character Bergman switches almost entirely to the manner of presenting a social document, according to which Berit is doomed, at least in her present environment. Her final words, "And soon it will be summer," imply a central thought in Bergman's films from the early fifties: that in summertime life becomes simple and pure. In *Port of Call*, however, there is nothing to warrant such a feeling. Attached to a realistic and gloomy picture is a romantic denouement, a piece of wishful thinking. In terms of the film's own premises an escape to a foreign country, not to an exotic never-never land but to a different social milieu, would have been a more realistic course of action.

An inability to fuse an objective environment with the inner life of his characters aligns *Port of Call* with most of Bergman's early works for the screen. Yet, the film is impressive and new from a cinematic point of view. It is the first film in which Bergman seems to have freed himself from a static, theatrical approach to his subject. It is true that the film as a whole lacks strong movement, but each individual scene uses a mobile camera that makes the utmost in absorbing the activities on ships, piers, and factories. Although such contemporary social realism is seldom used again in Bergman's films, *Port of Call* made him discover what a flexible and dynamic instrument the camera can be. Soon afterwards came his breakthrough as a film-maker,—*The Devil's Wanton*—and his first appearance as *cinéma d'auteur* (director of his own script).

IV The Devil's Wanton (Fängelse)

The plot: An old mathematics teacher gets an idea for a film and tells it to a former pupil of his, a film director. The film is to begin with a proclamation by the Devil (a later Bergman film, *The Devil's Eye,* actually has such a beginning): Human life is an inferno. The Devil will reign by maintaining things as they are.

The plot now turns to the home of Tomas, a young author whose marriage has brought him to the verge of suicide and murder. The director tells him of the teacher's idea, and Tomas in turn describes a meeting with a prostitute, Birgitta-Carolina. The action is visualized; the "real" film begins, focusing on the young girl and demonstrating the schoolteacher's thesis. Mixing cruel naturalistic details with expressionistic dream sequences, Bergman tells of a rendezvous between Tomas and Birgitta-Carolina in an old attic. There the young couple try to retrieve their lost childhood, symbolized by an old silent farce they find in a movie projector. At the same time, the short strip is a commentary on Birgitta-Carolina's and Tomas' present situation: the burlesque film shows people who are being chased by the police and by Death.

In the attic Birgitta-Carolina falls asleep and has a nightmare: she meets Tomas and lays her head on his chest only to find that he is a stranger with a death mask. Coming upon a bathtub she sees a doll bobbing in the water; a hand lifts up the doll but it changes into a fish, which the hand twists and breaks. Through her dream Birgitta-Carolina reenacts an earlier surrender of her infant to the sister of a pimp who has drowned it.

Next, the camera follows Tomas to the harbor. He sees a dead bird and kicks it into the water, an anticipation of Birgitta-Carolina's death. He then reads a poster advertising a weekly magazine with the headline: "Why did you go?" Here the film cuts to Birgitta-Carolina. After a meeting with a former lover who burns her wrist with a cigarette butt, she runs down to the basement and commits suicide, using a knife that a small boy has left there. Birgitta-Carolina has let her child die; now she dies through the involuntary assistance of a child. Such melodramatic irony through parallel structure is frequently used in the film.

The camera moves back to Tomas who returns in the early morning to his wife. He has never loved Birgitta-Carolina, but meeting her has had a liberating influence on him. She has acted out his frustration and suffered in his place.

The film ends as we go back to the director's studio. The teacher arrives to ask him his opinion of the original idea. The director answers that it would be impossible to make a film like that. It would have to end on a question mark, and to whom should the question (of guilt) be put, since there is no God?—

It may be true as Jacques Siclier has pointed out that even a fairly detailed synopsis of the film does it great injustice and makes us forget the superiority of the camera to the film's theme and story.[6] In its swift cutting from one milieu to another, in its mixture of the burlesque and melodramatic, in its use of posters and headlines, the film displays a certain technical boldness of a kind that Jean-Luc Godard was later to push to the extreme in a work like *Pierrot le fou*. But such a style calls for greater playfulness than Bergman's heavy-handed approach to his subject permits. His tear-dripping story overshadows his craftsmanship, and rather than noticing his sensitive use of camera to suggest dramatic movement we begin to question the authenticity of his view of life as presented in *The Devil's Wanton*. Bergman calls the film "a morality play for the cinema," but what he presents is a gloomy naturalistic milieu that is too selective to represent the total vision of a world of moral absolutes. The fate of Birgitta-Carolina is by no means unbelievable, but it is too extreme to serve the normative function of an action in a morality play.

Yet, as a piece of heightened reality, of nightmare, *The Devil's Wanton* is at times very successful. In the dream sequences we find a dramatic and plastic reality which is practically autonomous, so that the verbal content is at best a variation of an image or movement, at worst a superfluous tautology. A mood of imprisonment and frustration (the film's Swedish title means "prison") is conveyed by the camera as it transmits long, corridor-like shots of narrow streets; interiors showing apartments cluttered with furniture as if to leave less space to the people in them; close-ups of beds on which the bars of the bedstead suggest a prison window; a concentration on details that reinforce a sense of personal isolation.[7] Yet, the symbolism of the film emerges through the total action of a sequence rather than through an individually composed shot. It is a development that was to be part of Bergman's strength as a film-maker and one that he would follow until he made *The Silence*.

The dream sequences, suggesting Birgitta-Carolina's guilt feelings in surrendering her child to "the hands of death," foreshadow the inward, self-probing movement of Bergman's later films. But it is no more than an indication. Self-pity or identification with the young prevents Bergman from letting his characters face themselves and assume their share of responsibility. In *The Devil's Wanton* frustration and unhappiness are not partly self-inflicted (as, for instance, *in The Seventh Seal* and *Wild Strawberries*) but are brought on by the adult world surrounding the main characters. As in all of Bergman's early films, hope still resides in man and woman joined together: Tomas' reunion with his wife at the end has a light touch. But the lonely individual is doomed.

Hence, from a thematic point of view *The Devil's Wanton* does not denote a new phase in Bergman's production but rather a summing up of his early adolescent position. But only a year later Bergman admitted: *"The Devil's Wanton"* represents a point of view that I have been forced to give up." [8]

CHAPTER 4

The World of Women

—"The world of women is my universe."

MARIANNE HÖÖK has rightly observed that *Three Strange Loves* (1949) gave Bergman new impulses in his conception of women; he became aware of the loneliness of women, of a female hell.[1] Or more precisely, he stepped out of his egocentric treatment of male *Weltschmerz* and began to produce a whole line of films in which the point of view is feminine: *Three Strange Loves* (*Törst*), *Illicit Interlude* (*Sommarlek*), *Divorced* (*Frånskild*), *Secrets of Women* (*Kvinnors väntan*), *Monika* (*Sommaren med Monika*), *Dreams* (*Kvinnodröm*), and *Brink of Life* (*Nära livet*). Of these I have omitted from this discussion *Divorced* because it is an insignificant film, and *Monika* because it reiterates the mood and setting of *Illicit Interlude*, except where the voice of the original author breaks through (the script was adapted from a novel by Per Anders Fogelström).

I Three Strange Loves (Törst)

The plot: An incompatible married couple, Ruth and Bertil, are in the compartment of a train traveling from Basel to Stockholm and traversing bomb-devastated Germany (the time is 1947). In flashbacks we learn the reasons for their unhappiness. Ruth has become sterile by forced abortion after an affair with an officer. For a while she has been absorbed in her work as a ballet dancer, but now she is getting too old to perform.

Next, we meet Viola, the "other woman" in Bertil's life. We follow her story during a lonely midsummer evening in Stockholm. There is a suggestion that lesbianism—like Ruth's abortion leading to a sterile death-in-life—accounts for her isolation, but Viola is also victimized by a sadistic psychiatrist, a remnant of the diabolic world in Bergman's earlier films.

As Ruth and Bertil approach the end of their journey, the two plots coalesce. Viola is driven to suicide; Bertil's and Ruth's quarrel reaches a climax when Bertil dreams that he has murdered his wife. Waking up in a cold sweat he finds Ruth alive. Although her incessant arguments have driven him to desperation, he does not want to lose her:

BERTIL: I don't want to be alone and independent. That's worse.
RUTH: Than what?
BERTIL: Than the hell we are living in. After all, we have each other.—

Three Strange Loves is Bergman's first film to concentrate on a middle-aged neurotic couple rather than on adolescents. It is a Strindbergian drama of the sexes, based on a collection of short stories by Birgit Tengroth. In the original these are independent, but in Bergman's film they are tied together. One story, *Travel with Arethusa,* is used as the main plot while the others form the flashbacks and memories of the central characters.

Ruth's and Bertil's journey through Europe is as symbolic as the sisters' stopover in the war-threatened city in *The Silence.* As they look out at the desolate and ravaged landscape, they are not preoccupied by any humanitarian or pacifist problems. What they experience is the ruin of their marriage, and their journey is a nightmare, symbolically reflected in but morally independent of the world outside. Their parts are played by the same actors who did Tomas and his wife in *The Devil's Wanton.* Bergman may have wanted to suggest that the hopeful reunion of the married couple in the earlier film has turned into a satanic relationship. Hell is now a private affair between husband and wife; marriage means confinement and frustration for both parties. The narrow compartment of the train is as fitting a metaphor for the collapse of married life as is the isolated fortress in Strindberg's *The Dance of Death.* One can also understand why *Three Strange Loves* has been called Bergman's version of Sartre's *No Exit.*[2]

Three Strange Loves illustrates in parallel actions two depressing possibilities open to people of Ruth's, Bertil's, and Viola's kind: self-destruction or a desperate form of fellowship. As in Strindberg's dramas, marriage is not based on sexual compatibil-

ity or loving concern but on a mutual need. Marriage is a shield
against loneliness.

The strength of the film lies in its portrait of the married couple,
and in particular of Ruth. Close-ups reveal a strong sympathy for
her tortured face, but other images stress her sloppiness: there are
heaps of cigarette butts on her table; the bed is unmade and she
herself half-dressed. In skillful shots Bergman presents her vora-
ciously eating a stale sandwich, cutting a sausage with a razor
blade, and performing a grimacing pantomime in the mirror as
she examines one of her teeth. Her husband's mounting irritation
is set off against his inborn pedantry: after each quarrel he carefully combs his hair.

Three Strange Loves is a film in which the faces are often more
expressive than the dialogue. The ending, *i.e.*, the reconciliation
between Ruth and Bertil, suffers from being largely verbalized.
On the other hand, Bergman carries at times visualization too far:
in the dream sequence in which Bertil kills Ruth, the shock effect
overshadows Bertil's agony. One might compare this ending with
that of a later Bergman film, *The Naked Night,* in which the
clown Frost *tells* us of an important dream he has had, while the
main characters, Albert and Anne, come together without a
word.[3]

A claustrophobic setting and excessive heat underscore the tension between the main characters in *Three Strange Loves*. The
only happy memory shows us Ruth in Sweden at midsummer:
open space and pleasant warm weather are here used in contrast
to the hot, closed quarters of the train. But the northern summer is
a fitting frame only for young lovers. For someone like Viola it
will merely accentuate a feeling of being an outsider.

The summer motif is somewhat of a cliché in Swedish literature
and film. The short Swedish summer with its intense light has
become a metaphor for carefree liberty; pure, idyllic living; brief
moments of happiness. For those who live on memories it means
dreams of a lost paradise.

II Illicit Interlude (Sommarlek)

Bergman's most sophisticated use of the summer motif occurs in
his comedy *Smiles of a Summer Night,* but his warmest and most
personal rendering of the summer theme is *Illicit Interlude,*[4] as is

also reflected in one of his own statements about the making of the film: "I made *Sommarlek* with my heart. The plot had to do with the best there is: Summer vacation in the archipelago and The First Great Love, two manifestations rather fresh in my memory, but already seeming incredibly far away—yes, experienced in another and happier life." [5]

Illicit Interlude was originally a short story that Bergman wrote when he was seventeen. Later the script went through a series of revisions. In 1945 Bergman was ready to make the film; the title was then *Sentimental Journey*. But the final version was not completed until 1951, and then with the help of Herbert Grevenius.

The plot: The film begins and ends at the Opera in Stockholm. David, a journalist, is waiting for Mari, an aging ballerina, but leaves as Mari is occupied with a dress rehearsal of *Swan Lake*. Mari's uncle Erland has sent her an old diary, which he has stolen years earlier when Mari stayed on an island in the archipelago. His intention is to destroy Mari by opening in her the wound of a lost love.

Mari begins to read the diary and returns in her memories to the island where she spent a brief summer with her lover Henrik. There are three flashbacks, the first and second of which are hesitant and idyllic in tone, culminating when Mari takes Henrik to her secret wild strawberry patch on a hillside by the sea. The third sequence is tragic and contains, from the beginning, a foreboding of death: Mari visits Henrik's house; in an arbor an old lady is playing chess with the minister; she has breast cancer; yet, to the minister she is an interesting study object: "However absurd it may sound, I have a strange feeling that I am sitting here in the company of death itself." It is a scene anticipating the chess game between Antonius Block and Death in *The Seventh Seal*.

The next morning death puts an end to Henrik's and Mari's love. In an exuberant leap from a cliff Henrik accidentally hits his head on an underwater rock and is killed. (In the original script, Henrik was killed when he fell off the roof of Mari's cottage; the change was perhaps made in order to stress an ironic contrast between the happy bathing scenes in the earlier flashbacks and the final, fateful one.)

Mari is not a recluse dwelling on her memories; she is a hard-working ballerina who has escaped from pain into art, following the advice of her teacher: "You are dancing. That is your formula.

Stick to that, or things will turn out badly." Her problem, however, is not that of choosing between art and life, but of finding a
way to integrate the two. That she succeeds is suggested in the
end: David and Mari embrace because "the dead man and the
living finally form a synthesis, that of feeling." [6] The background
for this scene is the white luminous setting from *Swan Lake's*
opening night; the final shot shows us Mari dancing back upon
the stage.—

In an early scene in *Illicit Interlude* we see a close-up of Mari
alone; only half her face is visible. A sound stirs her and she seems
to sense that the dead Henrik is in the hallway outside. Going out
she sees a strange figure emerge in the background—the choreog-
rapher in his role as magician in the ballet *Coppelia*. The scene
then returns to normality. But in this brief sequence Bergman has
telescoped the essential aim of the film: to make Mari face the
past, to make the spirit of the dead present in her, so that she can
finally overcome it and go on living. [7]

The end of Henrik's life meant the end of summer and the end
of Mari as a carefree being. Bitterly she has upbraided heaven for
letting the accident occur. She has mentioned God by name, but
He has remained an abstraction to her. Only through the catharsis
of a journey back into the past can Mari free herself from the
deadening impact of the meaningless philosophy she has accepted
as hers when Henrik was killed. Her return to life is gradual. Between the second and third flashbacks she pays a visit to Uncle
Erland, who embodies a deterministic and cynical point of view.
Finding him in his darkened summer villa, Mari disavows and
criticizes him; their parting is final. But Mari can now relive the
most painful episode in her past without being destroyed by it.

The mood of nostalgia and memory that permeates *Illicit Interlude* is transmitted to us through both setting and form. Marianne
Höök has pointed out that a summer milieu such as Bergman depicts in the film no longer exists: "One has to go back one generation, to Bergman's childhood, to find such aspects of high society,
la grande bourgeoisie that lived in manor-like country estates,
playing Chopin in the parlor-room." [8] Yet the archaic is only part
of the milieu. All the permanent seasonal attributes of the northern summer are used: tranquil water, island scenery, glittering
sunshine, and lingering twilight. The effect is an idealized, yet
factual rendering of a story of young love. [9] The camera is used

very sensitively to emphasize this; the pictorial beauty of the film
has not been surpassed in any other Bergman picture. Prolonged
shots in counter-light and "the presence of two scenes simultaneously during a longer period than one is accustomed to give the
film a lingering melancholy which suits the subject." [10] The camera
also helps establish nature, not only as symbol and backdrop but
as an active part in the film. Black naked trees of autumn introduce Mari's return to the island where the essential conflict between past and present begins to unfold. The idyllic mood of the
two early flashbacks is reflected in large, romantic pictures, while,
in the tragic sequence, dark clouds foreshadow the death of
Henrik.

Illicit Interlude is superior to anything Bergman had done earlier for the screen. It does not employ the bold, experimental technique of *The Devil's Wanton*—usually a favorite among Bergman
fans—but it is unique in his production so far, in that it achieves
unity of content as well as formal balance. Unlike *The Devil's
Wanton* and to some extent *Three Strange Loves, Illicit Interlude*
is not cluttered by subplots that are never developed; nor is the
dialogue overlaced with pretentious rhetoric as in some of Bergman's more ambitious films.

The fusion of content and style can best be illustrated by comparing Bergman's use of the flashback in this film with the earlier
Three Strange Loves. Ruth's memories had mainly the function of
explaining her present hysteria and her nostalgic longing for a lost
happiness. But they did not influence her present life; she remained a static personality throughout the film, and her defeated,
deterministic point of view threatened to destroy the film's dramatic structure. By contrast, the flashbacks in *Illicit Interlude* are
used so that present and past mingle and finally fuse. When that
happens the main character has suffered and come through: a
new life can begin for Mari. It is not the happy ending of *Illicit
Interlude,* of course, that makes it a better film but the fact that
Mari is conceived as a dynamic and changing character and that
the very structure of the film underscores this. It is no exaggeration, therefore, when Eugene Archer claims that with *Illicit Interlude* Bergman reaches maturity as a film-maker.[11] From now on he
will create "few films which are not masterful in their evocation
of mood and movement, the principal ingredients of a cinematic
style." [12]

III   Secrets of Women (Kvinnors väntan)

In Swedish films before 1950 two standard types of women appeared: the vamp and the folksy country girl, the former inevitably dressed in black lingerie, the latter the epitome of health and innocence. This schematic dichotomy influenced the early Bergman although in his films the vamp is portrayed as the social victim rather than the embodiment of sin (*The Devil's Wanton, Port of Call, A Ship to India*). The country-girl type becomes in Bergman's world the innocent girl of summer; her first appearance is the *young* Mari in *Illicit Interlude*. She will return in later films (as Sara in *Wild Strawberries*, Mia in *The Seventh Seal*, Karin in *The Virgin Spring*, Annette Egerman in *Smiles of a Summer Night*). She displays some variations: carefree exuberance, coquettishness, or timidity, but she always has an idealistic or naive approach to life and refuses to accept the (realistic) compromises of an older generation of women.

Bergman's film from 1952, *Secrets of Women* is conceived as an object lesson for such a young girl.

The plot: The film is built up around a narrative frame. A group of married women sit in a country cottage and wait for their husbands' return. One of them, Annette (the oldest), begins to express doubts that their marriages will stand up to the close scrutiny of a long summer vacation. She concludes that all marriages are disappointing and that a woman's consolation lies either "in Jesus or the grandchildren." The others concur, each telling a revealing episode from her married life. Thereupon the husbands arrive, while the teen-age sister of one of the married women elopes with a young man, heedless of the stories she has heard. As the boat with the young lovers sets out on the water, the boy's father says: "Let them leave. They will come back one day. . . . Let them profit from their summer. They will know soon enough the wounds, the wisdom of life, and other silly matters."—

Secrets of Women is an episodic film much in vogue at the time. Its narrative method gives us more variety than depth, a series of female destinies rather than a concentrated analysis of one individual. Bergman is to use the same approach in *Smiles of a Summer Night* and *Brink of Life*.

Technically the film is composed of different elements as if Bergman had wanted to give each story its own distinctive style, suitable to the vision of each narrator. The first story deals with Rakel, the most complex of the women, and is a screen adaptation of Bergman's play *Rachel and the Cinema Doorman*. The emphasis has now shifted from the intruder Kaj to Rakel and her husband Eugen. As in the play they are reconciled in the end. What dictates Rakel's decision to remain with her husband is a maternal feeling which is born in her when she sees his helplessness: "I understood that he was only a child and that it was my duty to watch over him." Yet, her maternal love is by no means unselfish, for as Peter Cowie has pointed out there is something in Rakel herself that prefers resignation to emotional outlet, an erotic immaturity that leads her to develop direcly from tomboy (she is dressed in an overall) to substitute mother.[13]

While Rakel's story is somewhat theatrically conceived, the second episode is partly realistic, partly expressionistic. It is composed around a flashback within a flashback: the subconscious within a memory. Marta, a relatively young woman, remembers the moment she gave birth to her child. Camera angle, montage, and shrieking sound effects express her anguish. Then realistic shots of the baby's arrival begin to fuse with Marta's nightmarish visions of a cancan dance in a Parisian nightclub where she and the father of the child first met.

By reliving the past—like Mari in *Illicit Interlude*—Marta can finally accept the baby in joy. She subsequently marries her spineless lover, realizing that he can have no identity without her. Like Rakel, Marta comes to her husband as a mother and not as a lover. That this is what gives women their strength to accept and endure is demonstrated in the third and final episode, a classic in Bergman's production, in which the problem of directing in the closed space of an elevator is solved by the use of a mirror on one wall. Never before had the mirror been used so skillfully by Bergman, although it played an important part in, for instance, *Three Strange Loves* and *Illicit Interlude*. The mirror has a varied function in Bergman's films; it is an instrument of reflection in which the characters interrogate themselves. It has seldom a mere narcissistic purpose; it is as much a cruel witness as an object for self-admiration. It measures the course of time, the coming of old age; it registers the marks of suffering and loneliness in a face. At other times, the mirror serves to deform reality and anticipate scenes in which the actors are exposed to humiliating experiences. In *Three*

Strange Loves the mirror is used to show a face in both profile and *en face*, which gives the episode both variety and concentration. As Jean Collet has remarked, the technique is a transposition of cubist painting to the screen.[14]

The third episode concerns a successful businessman and his sophisticated but neglected wife. During the night they are forced to spend in an elevator, they taunt each other with their infidelities and then grow intimate for the first time in years. They decide to go on a second honeymoon, but when the elevator is repaired in the morning, the husband discovers that he is late for an appointment and rushes off to work, forgetting the entire incident. The wife muses over the fate of women and accepts her husband's shortcomings with good humor. Again the point of view emphasizes the childishness of the man.

To Bergman marriage is not a social phenomenon or a religious institution. It is a psychological necessity existing outside all moral conventions. The disillusionment that marriage will bring can only be alleviated by the arrival of children. Even for the childless couple, the woman must accept a maternal role in the marriage. The most bitter experience in *Secrets of Women* is that of Annette, who never tells her story but reveals the bankruptcy of her marriage as she confesses: "I cannot tear out his [my husband's] eyes to make him blind and dependent upon me. I cannot even take him in my arms and rock him when I feel that he is sad and suspicious."

IV Dreams (Kvinnodröm)

As if to prove that the experiences of the housewives in *Secrets of Women* were not conditioned by their married status, Bergman made another film, *Dreams* (1955), in which he told of the disillusionment of two unmarried professional women.

The plot: A fashion manager, Susanne, and her young model, Doris, travel to Gothenburg on business. Susanne looks up her lover, Lobelius, who wishes to annul his marriage but discloses that he is economically dependent upon his wife. During a crucial meeting at the hotel where Susanne is staying, Marta Lobelius arrives and unmasks her husband completely by revealing his lack of will-power. Susanne is cured of her passion when she realizes that Loebelius does not correspond to her image of him. Later she rejects his suggestion regarding a future liaison.

Meanwhile Doris has been strolling about in the city, nourish-
ing her particular dream: beautiful clothes and jewelry, a big car,
and an expensive house. She meets her prince in the form of an
elderly gentleman, Consul Sönderby, who takes her to the Fun
Fair. Later, in Sönderby's home, the rendezvous is interrupted by
the consul's daughter, who reveals her father's stinginess and egotism. Doris then decides to return to her boyfriend Palle, whom
she had left behind in Stockholm.—

Dreams is a film in which one senses the influence of the stage;
it is constructed according to the dramatic rules of exposition,
crisis, and denouement. The introductory scenes, which are too
complete and autonomous, show us Susanne's and Doris' business
milieu and depict the former's rather desperate mood. The film
really begins when the camera starts to follow the two women
during their adventures in Gothenburg.

The film is composed along two parallel actions, which are independent of each other and could have been made into separate
films. Thematically, however, they are closely related and reinforce each other; they illustrate the failure of Susanne and Doris
as well as the men they encounter to realize the dreams each one
of them nurtures.

The four main characters represent three generations: youth
(Doris); approaching middle age (Susanne and Lobelius); approaching old age (Consul Sönderby). But as Harry Schein has
pointed out, the difference in age between the characters is of
anecdotal rather than dramatic consequence.[15] In earlier films
Bergman had suggested that dreams and illusions belong to the
young; in *Dreams* he implies that they can motivate people
throughout their lives.

Susanne's dream is to marry, to have a home and children. Lobelius, on the other hand, dreams of freedom and independence.
Doris displays the fantasies of a teen-age egotist, but her willingness to exploit the Consul's generosity is counterbalanced by his
equally selfish motives: *he* dreams of using Doris, who resembles
his dead wife, as a mirror in which he can contemplate his past in
a glorified light.

The two episodes have a rather similar structure: the woman
meets a man; the illusions they maintain about each other are
shattered by an "intruder," in both cases a realistic, somewhat cal-

culating woman whose strength is her lack of compassion and her knowledge that she controls the man by her insight into his weaknesses. Both Marta Lobelius and Sönderby's daughter display an ice-cold logic. In Bergman's world they represent a destructive rather than norm-giving element. His sympathy is on the side of the dreamers.

Dreams contains various cinematic styles, each one aimed at conveying the mood of the central character in a particular sequence. One of the opening scenes, depicting Susanne's depression, achieves its aspect of nightmare by the use of the weird, rainswept window of a compartment as a mirror. At the same time, Bergman lets all the natural sounds from the onrushing train accompany the shots of Susanne's reflection in the glass. Both the pictorial and the sound elements are naturalistic, but the juxtaposition of them is not. Rather, the effect is one of a fragmented, yet distilled reality, such as we meet in our dreams. One might compare this technique to the completely objectified, matter-of-fact rendering of reality in the unmasking scenes. Here the coolness and detachment of Marta Lobelius and Sönderby's daughter dictate the style. The meeting between Doris and the Consul, finally, is filmed with an impressionistic technique to suit Doris' dreams. Here Bergman makes the utmost use of the unreality of the Fun Fair; the major sequence takes place on the roller coaster and contrasts Doris' thoughtless exuberance with the Consul's forced vitality. The setting corresponds not only to Doris' romantic temperament but also to the Consul's fear, culminating in his collapse at the end of the ride.

V Brink of Life (Nära livet)

Jean Collet has observed that in *Dreams* the sound effects often tell more than direct communication.[16] Bergman proved early that he is a master in the use of natural sounds. On the other hand, he has always been very economical in his use of music. His next major film about women, *Brink of Life* (1958), lacks music completely, except at one point when a nurse's radio is heard. The reason, according to Bergman, was that he "wanted the style to be as bare as possible." [17] The natural sounds in the film support his intention to make a realistic, almost documentary picture. Unlike *Dreams* the sounds in *Brink of Life* contrast rather than express

the emotions of the women involved and emphasize the gulf between their joy and anguish, and the matter-of-fact atmosphere of
the hospital.

The plot: Brink of Life tells of three women who meet in the
maternity ward of a hospital. The oldest of them, Cecilia Ellius,
is a professional woman who has had a miscarriage. The second
woman, Stina, is a healthy-looking matron who seems created
solely for the role of reproducer of the species. Her labor is difficult, however, and the baby is stillborn.

The third woman is a nineteen-year-old girl, Hjördis. She is not
married and insists upon an abortion. But her experiences in the
hospital convince her that she should give birth to the child even
though it is against the wishes of its father. Hjördis is a Bergman
addition to the plot, which was based on a short story by Ulla
Isaksson, taken from her collection *Dödens faster* (*The Aunt of
Death*).—

Brink of Life is so meticulous in its factual rendering of hospital
life as to be almost a nonfictional film. Bergman made use of a
medical counselor and researched in a hospital for a long time
before starting the picture: "It was a difficult job and really more
in the nature of a study." [18] In keeping with his striving for an
ascetic approach, Bergman uses no flashbacks, no dream sequences, no expressionistic photography, and his actresses wear
no makeup. The setting throughout the entire film is the naked,
antiseptic hospital milieu, and most of the action is confined to
one room.

That *Brink of Life* approaches the documentary is corroborated
by the fact that it does not attempt to make well-rounded stories
out of the three women's experiences. The film has no definite
ending. It is a rather static movie which relies on close-ups and
swift cutting to create tension and drama. What Bergman wants
to capture—and here the film transcends the aim of the documentary—is the inner life of the three women in the ward. As Peter
Cowie has suggested, the film's *raison d'être* lies "in the memory
of an intense episode that has racked and finally calmed the principal characters." [19] Bergman depicts for us life at a given instant
—women facing childbirth—suggesting perhaps the classic existential situation in which a man facing a firing squad has time to
change the whole meaning of his life.[20] Giving birth is treated as

a phenomenon (rather than a function) and in Bergman's world it is as inexplicable and lonely a moment as the moment of death.

Brink of Life bears a certain resemblance to *Secrets of Women:* in the maternity ward, as in the kitchen of the summer house, women come together, not to gossip but to confess. In *Secrets of Women,* however, the individual episodes are handed to us in mechanical flashbacks and in an effort to kill time, giving them nevertheless a quality of *Kaffeeklatsch* memoirs, while in *Brink of Life* the women unfold their thoughts and feelings under the pressure and agony of the present. Here Bergman does not need the flashback technique, for the men's visits to the maternity ward furnish enough background material to explain the women's plights.

The three fathers are responsible for the women's attitude toward childbirth. Stina's husband is a solid, down-to-earth man whose uncomplicated nature stands in direct relation to Stina's joyful expectancy. Ellius, Cecilia's husband, is a Bergman intellectual, a nihilistic type that frequently is to play the role of devil archetype and succeeds the earlier father-tyrant figure in Bergman's films. Ellius does not wish to have children, which has created a neurotic attitude in Cecilia toward the baby she has been expecting. She blames herself for its loss, but Bergman suggests that Cecilia may have desired its death for fear of her husband's resentment of the child.

The father of Hjördis' child does not appear. His denial of responsibility leads Hjördis to reject the thought of a baby. When she later decides to keep her child, she is made to appear as a contrast to Cecilia Ellius, as a person who braves the destructive influence of a life-denying man (in this respect she anticipates Marianne, the daughter-in-law in *Wild Strawberries*). But her addition to the script also adds an ironic twist to the story: while Cecilia loses the child that she claims she has desired, Hjördis cannot at first get rid of the baby she does not want. Their situation illustrates the main philosophical mood of the film: that "chance becomes the deciding factor for the weal of man." [21] Stina's experience, finally, confirms this most strongly: the death of her baby is inexplicable. No subconscious wishes or fears are at play; medical negligence cannot be blamed. It is merely blind fate ruling supreme.

None of the works discussed in this chapter are usually listed among Bergman's major films, with the possible exception of *Illicit Interlude*. Yet, each film is important as a technical achievement. One admires these works for their finished style and for the cinematic form adapted to the vision they want to convey. When Bergman leaves the world of women and returns to male protagonists, his form is to become bolder, his questioning deeper. The result is more puzzling and intriguing films but also more uneven ones. If one prefers unified, although less splendid works, the films with Woman as central consciousness will seem superior.

CHAPTER 5

The Seventh Seal

B ERGMAN'S film from 1957—*The Seventh Seal*—is based upon his earlier play *Wood Painting*. It is set in fourteenth-century Sweden, and tells of a crusader's quest for God.

The plot: Weary and disillusioned, Antonius Block and his squire Jöns have returned from the Holy Land. Upon their arrival in Sweden they learn that the country is ravaged by the bubonic plague. Death comes in person to claim the crusader but is challenged by him to a game of chess. Antonius Block gets a respite: as long as the game goes on, he is to be free to continue his search for knowledge of God and the meaning of life.

Setting off again on their homebound journey, Antonius Block and Jöns meet a number of people who all experience a great sense of immanence, for they know that they may die soon. Among them are a smith and his unfaithful wife; Raval, a sadistic priest; a church painter who lives to frighten people by painting realistic pictures of the dance of death; a witch, Tyan, who seems to welcome death; and a troupe of actors whose performance is interrupted by a train of flagellants carrying huge wooden crosses. From time to time Death intercepts the Knight in order to make a move on the chessboard. On one such occasion Antonius Block distracts Death, so that a young couple, Jof and Mia, can escape the plague with their infant son Mikael. As a result, however, the crusader loses the game and when he reaches his home, Death comes to claim him, his wife, and his company.—

The Seventh Seal begins with the sound track transmitting the resonant voices of a church choir. Then the singing suddenly stops and there is absolute silence. The camera moves in upon the Knight who is waking up, and glides over the face of Jöns, who lies asleep with gaping mouth. The time is early morning; the light is gray and nature seems to lie in a coma.

After a prayer, the Knight stares into the morning sun, "which

wallows up from the misty sea like some bloated dying fish." High
above the infinite ocean a sea gull is floating on its wings. "Its cry
is weird and restless." This scene is not merely a piece of cinematic exposition; it is a thematic prelude: in the image of the
crying bird seen against a sky which is "a dome of lead," Bergman
telescopes the Knight's hopeless search for God, who remains distant and silent.

A voice, which now begins to read a brief passage from the
Revelation of St. John the Divine, speaks directly to the Knight,
who fails to understand its message. But the passage also puts the
title of the film into context. God's Book of Secrets is to be imag-
ined as a scroll of parchment with seven seals. Not until the seventh seal is broken will man know the secret of life: "And when he
had opened the seventh seal, there was a silence in heaven about
the space of half an hour." Bergman's film can be regarded as a
visualization of that half hour during which man may prepare
himself for the ultimate truth.

As the voice reads, the camera shifts its angle; high aerial shots
from the cliffs above the beach depict an absolutely desolate
country. As Peter Cowie has pointed out, "we seem to be in a
mythic country of death." [1] Thus, we are prepared for the actual
figure of Death, which appears next on the screen. With his im-
mobile, white face and wide, black coat, the actor's personification
of Death suggests a Grand Guignol figure. The Knight, however,
is never surprised by his meeting with Death and, except once,
Bergman never lets Death be visible to the audience while being
invisible to Antonius Block. Thus the theatrical suspense is toned
down rather than emphasized. [2]

Although the Knight's quest is medieval, his skeptic and anxious
temper is modern. To help justify such an anachronism Bergman
claims that the medieval world depicted in *The Seventh Seal* is
basically a historical metaphor for our own world threatened by
atomic destruction: "In my film the crusader returns from the
Crusades as the soldier returns from the war today. In the Middle
Ages, men lived in terror of the plague. Today they live in fear of
the atomic bomb. *The Seventh Seal* is an allegory with a theme
that is quite simple: man, his eternal search for God, with death
as his only certainty." [3]

Bergman's use of the term "allegory" should be taken in a general rather than medieval sense, being a story in which the spirit-

ual content is set forth in a concrete action and with characters whose movements are realistic but whose basic function is that of abstract symbols. Many have objected, however, that the film is composed of too many disparate elements: Bergman borrows freely from old frescoes he had seen as a child, which accounts for such allegorized sequences as Jof's vision of Mia in the traditional rose garden of the Virgin Mary, and Death sawing off the tree (of life) in which Skat, the actor, has taken refuge. Also, the idea of the chess game stems from medieval allegories. But the central characters fall outside such a pattern and cannot be classified according to any traditional symbolism. To some critics this means that they function only on a personal plane: ". . . the knight, his squire, the strolling players and the other characters deployed here, are not *true* symbols. That is to say, what they symbolize is not universally recognizable." [4]

Philosophically, *The Seventh Seal* departs from medieval allegory in two respects: the metaphysical uncertainty that characterizes Bergman's film has little in common with the *a priori* assumption of an orderly universe, which underlies original allegory; and the central character in the prototypal allegory is not haunted by doubt; his problem is forgetfulness of God, and God emerges not as an enigma but as a father figure anxious to reach and save His straying child.

The philosophical mood of *The Seventh Seal* is related to the existentialist view that a human life is decided not in intellectual questioning but in the choice of action. To Jöns, the squire, who in spite of his cynical verbosity is compassionate in his deeds, the Knight is a fool who has wasted ten years of his life asking futile questions: "Ten years we sat in the Holy Land and let the snakes bite us, insects prick us, wild animals nip us, heathens slaughter us, the wine poison us, women give us lice, fleas feed on us, and fevers consume us, all to the glory of God. I'll tell you, our crusade was so stupid that only a real idealist could have invented it."

Jöns uses the term "idealist" in its original sense, i.e., a *man of ideas,* an intellectual. The crusade was bound to be meaningless because Antonius Block kept looking *beyond* it for some intellectual truth; he was not committed to the pilgrimage as a living act but to his own rational mind, which demanded that God show Himself in divine essence: "I want knowledge, not faith, not suppositions, but knowledge. I want God to stretch out his hand toward me, reveal Himself and speak to me." God as object should make the crusade a meaningful act.

The crusader's search was also destined to be blasphemous, for as in the archetypal legend of the Fall, a desire for ultimate knowledge is treason against God. Bergman has grasped the paradoxical implications of the old myth: man cannot seek full intellectual cognizance of God without disobeying Him; the more he tries to understand the nature of God the further he removes himself from God. Bergman illustrates this gradual alienation of man from the divine by depicting in the crusader a human being at first engaged in a holy enterprise but in the end willing to sell his soul to the Devil—could he only find him! For the Devil, the Knight argues with insane logic, must know God since he only exists in his opposition to God.

In the most brutal scene in the film, staged as a kind of exorcism, the crusader speaks to Tyan, who is about to be burnt as a witch:

KNIGHT: They say that you have been in league with the Devil.
TYAN: Why do you ask?
KNIGHT: Not out of curiosity, but for very personal reasons. I too want to meet him.
TYAN: Why?
KNIGHT: I want to ask him about God. He, if anyone, must know.
TYAN: You can see him any time.

But to the crusader the Devil as objectified reality remains as invisible and silent as God. Yet, Antonius Block fails to accept the implication that transcendental truth dwells in man himself, as potentialities of good and evil. Instead he tells Tyan: "I believe at times that to ask questions is the most important thing." The search has become his *raison d'être*.

Bergman juxtaposes the Knight's intellectual probing and his relationship with Jof and Mia, the visionary artist and the maternal woman, whose son one day will "perform the impossible trick of making a ball stand still in the air" (i.e., like Christ he will transcend nature). The traditional function of the crusader in medieval art was not as the colonizer of the Holy Land but as the protector of the Holy Family. Bergman's Knight performs the same service. But in saving Jof and his family by distracting Death's attention away from them, Antonius Block loses the game —and his life. It is a situation of ironic blasphemy: Man redeems Christ. On the other hand, it is an act made possible only because the crusader has caught a glimpse of love in his relationship with Jof and Mia. Perhaps the most crucial sequence in the film (and one that anticipates *Wild Strawberries*) is a low-keyed scene played on a sunny hillside, an idyllic picture of the Knight as he is being offered milk and wild strawberries by Mia. Strawberries are sometimes associated with the Virgin in late Northern iconography, but milk and wild strawberries are also private symbols in Bergman's world, the Eucharist in a communion between human beings.

It is on this occasion that the Knight vows: "I shall remember this moment. . . . I'll carry this memory between my hands as carefully as if it were a bowl filled to the brim with fresh milk. (He turns his face away and looks out toward the sea and the colorless gray sky). And it will be an adequate sign—it will be enough for me."

But the crusader does not keep his vow for long. The riddle of God continues to haunt him, and he is compelled to go on with his questioning. At one time it has brought about his fall from "paradise", his self-expulsion from a happy marriage. Antonius Block tells Mia of this loss of innocence: "We [my wife and I] were newly married and we played together. We laughed a great deal. I wrote songs to her eyes, to her nose, to her beautiful little ears. We went hunting together and at night we danced. The house was full of life."

The horribly negative aspect of the crusader's search becomes evident in the final sequence of the film, when Antonius Block is reunited with his wife. It is a strangely cold and detached meeting. The wife, whom we see for the first time, is cast as a woman of ascetic features. Later she officiates at a last supper, during which every sacramental element of redemption is absent and only the mood of impending doom prevails. As Death knocks at the castle door, the wife intones the words from the Book of Revelations.

The film does not end, however, on this pessimistic note but reiterates the permanent counterpoint of the story, which is a tension between those who willingly or by force succumb to death, and those who survive, representing the eternal values in life: compassion and generous love. This tension finds its resolution in the final scene: Jof, Mia, and the child look toward the horizon where they see all the other main characters who, led by Death, dance away to the country of shadows.

The figure of Death stands only on the threshold of the unknown; he is not a messenger, but merely a blind instrument. But he might be considered the focal point in the film. Like *Wood Painting, The Seventh Seal* concerns man's reactions in the face of eschatological matters. Almost all the characters can be linked to Death and evaluated acording to his influence over them. While Skat and Raval live as though Death did not exist, and Tyan and the flagellants as though nothing else existed, the Knight and Jöns carry on a resentful and challenging dialogue with Death. Although Jöns does not see the Knight's opponent in the chess game until the end, he is preoccupied with the thought of death; he is horrified by it and mocks it, but he is never indifferent to it. Throughout the film he is confronted with signs of Death's power. As he rides along in the morning, singing a bawdy song, he catches sight of a huddled figure on the ground. Turning it over, he stares at a skull. Later on he discusses the death motif with the church painter, and in spite of his own nonchalance ("This is squire Jöns. He grins at Death. . . .") he is so sickened by the pictures that he has to ask for a brandy. Jöns loves life; he is angered by the thought of annihilation, and his last words as he faces Death are words of remonstrance: "I shall be silent, but under protest."

Jöns is more than the hedonist he appears to be. Like Antonius Block he represents the consciousness of modern man. The Knight and his squire complement each other, and depict the skeptic personality facing a world where God is silent: one in futile introspection, the other in gallant action. They do not offer an alternative. All the film seems to say is that some people can live without illusions and still function as useful social beings, while others succumb to their need to believe and lose themselves in a search for God. At one point the Knight cries out: "Why can't I kill God within me? Why does He live on in this painful and humiliating way even though I curse Him and want to tear Him out of my heart? Why, in spite of everything is He a baffling reality that I can't shake off?" In this statement we sense again the modern temper of *The Seventh Seal:* the realization that moral will has given way to psychological needs—which excludes a possibility of choice.[5] Yet, both the Knight and Jöns are conceived as moral agents, and in this ambivalence Bergman again establishes his affinity with existentialist philosophy and its tenet according to which we must live as though we had a free will. The insoluble dilemma dramatized in the fate of Antonius Block also points to one of Ibsen's central themes: the curse (i.e., the moral judgment) that falls upon a man who *must* follow his calling.

There are several possible literary prototypes for *The Seventh Seal*. Bergman himself has mentioned George Bernanos' *The Diary of a Country Priest* as a source of inspiration. He also seems to have had the Faust figure in mind, both as it appeared in the stage version of *Ur-Faust* that Bergman produced at the Malmö City Theater shortly before he began to work on *The Seventh Seal*, and in Thomas Mann's *Dr. Faustus*, which had made a deep impression on him. Strindberg also lent his voice to the film. His historical play *The Saga of the Folkungs* (*Folkungasagan*) has a similar "cinematic" form: a panoramic setting, swift changes of scenes, abrupt "cuts" from mass scenes to intimate "close-ups." A train of flagellants appears in both works as well as quotations from the Revelation of St. John the Divine (in Strindberg from the Sixth Chapter, in Bergman from the Eighth).

With his fondness for musical analogies, Bergman has referred to *The Seventh Seal* as an oratorio. The comparison is suggestive but misleading if taken too literally. An oratorio is usually performed without action, costume or scenery. Bergman's film is full of visual splendor, and it has an excellent story. Furthermore, an oratorio is, as a rule, not only based upon a religious theme but is anchored in an unshaken faith in God and sung to his praise. *The Seventh Seal*, on the other hand, progresses in a mood of religious ambivalence. But no doubt Bergman never intended his "oratorio" to have more than a certain structural similarity to the musical genre: a composition for solo voices, chorus, and orchestra.

If one were to look for an analogy to *The Seventh Seal* in another art form, it might be more accurate to describe it as a cinematic tapestry, on which are interwoven the fates of many people, and where symbolic details sometimes confuse but always intrigue the spectator, the total effect being one of great plastic clarity.

While the visual impact of *The Seventh Seal* is tremendous, the film is marred by occasional verbal awkwardness, less noticeable in the English version which avoids the rhetorical resonance of some of the dialogue and translates the Knight's speech into colloquial language.

In *The Seventh Seal* movement is reserved for scenes that are visually descriptive, but spoken, introspective moments are not reflected by movement on the screen. This is in line with dramatic tradition: a Shakespearean soliloquy, for instance, is a physical pause. But Shakespeare's language possesses a visual power in itself, which Bergman's abstracted and prosaic language does not have. In later films Bergman develops—perhaps under the influence of TV—the close-up as an alternative to movement; the sensitive face of an actor or actress must then convey the feelings that the words alone cannot transmit.

As a film rather than a script, *The Seventh Seal* can be placed in the mainstream of Swedish cinematic tradition. Abroad it has often been mentioned together with Carl Dreyer's *Day of Wrath*, but visually *The Seventh Seal* has little in common with this film. Dreyer's style is stark and realistic, his rhythm slow and heavy. By comparison Bergman appears volatile and a little eclectic; his style oscillates between realistic scene-painting and abstracted symbolism, and aligns him with Victor Sjöström and classical Swedish films like *Terje Vigen* (1916) and *The Phantom Carriage* (1921). Like Sjöström, Bergman has gradually realized that the cinema can be a medium that lends itself to introspection and analysis with more flexibility than the theater.

As Bergman began to internalize earlier social and parental problems and transform them into questions of personal identity and/or faith—a development which no doubt has been crucial in shaping *la nouvelle vague* in the French cinema—the environment lost its autonomous quality of nature lyricism or realistic backdrop. In Bergman's early works, a human being may identify himself with the landscape, but nature still exists as an objective reality, possessing powers of its own. In *The Seventh Seal* scenery and weather (a night in the forest, a strong wind) are still used as ill omens, much the same as the dark clouds were used in *Illicit Interlude* to foreshadow the death of Henrik. In these instances the landscape serves as the artist's tool—one might call it Bergman's "Gothic quality."

But the landscape in *The Seventh Seal* is not only a ghost-like instrument; it emerges as a reflection of a state of mind, a metaphor of the self. The desolate landscape in the opening scenes of the film is an image of the isolation and despair of the Knight. The landscape which appears in Isak Borg's dreams in *Wild Strawberries* is a logical consequence of this tendency—a heritage from Victor Sjöström—to treat the surroundings as subjective image.

CHAPTER 6

Wild Strawberries

ONE final question keeps haunting us in *The Seventh Seal:* Can man achieve salvation, or in psychological terms, peace of mind? Some of the suggestions implied in the film are deeply ironic. The religious fanatics seek redemption by re-enacting the sufferings of Christ, a behavior which in anyone but Christ seems excessively proud and blasphemous. It is also the monks' god that leads them to burn Tyan as a witch and turns them into murderers. Only in Mia and Jof does Bergman depict people who know a god that is a *deus caritatis*. It is their voice, but without any direct reference to God, which is heard in Bergman's next film, *Wild Strawberries* (*Smultronstället*, 1957).

The plot: Wild Strawberries is set in our time and tells the story of Isak Borg, a 78-year-old physician who, when the film begins, is about to go to the University of Lund to receive his jubilee doctorate. The journey by car, which he makes with his daughter-in-law Marianne, becomes a journey back in time, not into historical time but into personal: Isak visits his childhood home; he dreams of his sweetheart Sara who rejected him for his sensual brother; and he stops to see his old mother, who sits like a frozen relic, absorbed in her bitterness and cut off from a family so large it could stand for humanity itself. Isak also has visions of his dead wife seeking elsewhere the love he was not able to give her. But as this past unfolds, it becomes part of the present: Sara, the sweetheart, returns as a young hitchhiker; the tortuous relationship between Isak and his wife is reflected in a miserable married couple whose car collides with Isak's; and the coldness of the heart which has characterized Isak's life, lives on in his son, Evald, who refuses to have children and demands that his pregnant wife have an abortion.

Gradually Isak gains insight into himself. By the time he reaches the end of his journey, he has come to realize his short-

comings. After the jubilee festivities he can rest peacefully, reconciled with his son and daughter-in-law.—

Isak Borg's search for peace and self-knowledge takes the outer
form of a journey through Sweden. He travels in a black, coffin-
like car, which Bergman uses to suggest Isak's withdrawal from
the world around him. Every time Isak steps out of the car, he in a
sense steps into a world that challenges him to commitment. All of
his experiences during the trip from Stockholm to Lund dramatize
the existentialist view which is the film's philosophical core: that
life is not a matter of merely being a spectator or submitting it to
cold analysis. In bringing about Isak's transformation, women
play a key role, for they are, like the heartbeat in one of Isak's
dreams, the living measure of existence. Both Marianne and
young Sara are in effect catalysts. Psychologically, the film is composed of a series of confrontations between Marianne and Isak,
and Sara and Isak. As he is drawn into their worlds, Isak begins to
examine his own life. He has the courage to revise it, but without
the women he could not have developed from atrophy and egotism to love and compassion.

In his totally scientific detachment from life, Isak Borg appears
to be Bergman's most clear-cut version of a cinematic Faust. But
whereas the classical Faust lusts after the universe of experience
out of insatiable desire, Isak Borg has pursued his scientific studies out of fear of himself. His withdrawal from the world is, in
effect, an attempt to flee from pain. He is an escapist Faust who
has lived in what Yeats called the artifice of eternity, a consoling
refuge created by the human mind beyond the agony and petti-
ness of natural existence. Isak's isolation is the self-created, secure
world of a man who has been unable to accept adulthood as a loss
of separateness. Young Isak lost his sweetheart Sara because he
could not give of himself. But in his inability, there was as much
fear as love of self.

In the course of the film Isak Borg learns not only to be a
human being concerned about the welfare of others, but, more
specifically, he learns to be a parent confronted by children. He
learns to care about his son and daughter-in-law, and he learns to
love young Sara whom he looks upon as a child. In accepting
parenthood, Isak can at last look back on his own childhood and
youth without bitterness. In his final vision, filled with nostalgia,
Isak returns to the strawberry patch of his childhood. In an earlier

dream he has watched in self-pity how Sara drops her basket of fresh strawberries as she loses her innocence to Isak's brother. But now young Sara takes old Isak by the hand and brings him to a nearby lake where he sees his parents sit in placid contentment, wearing clothes from the turn of the century. They wave to him and in responding to their gesture, Isak takes the last step out of his isolation, and through the love and harmony that he senses between his parents, he recognizes the pure passion that lies in parenthood. He has retrieved his innocence but he has also become an adult.

Although *Wild Strawberries* does not treat any problem of faith, it is conceived as a symbolic pilgrimage, as a form of penance. The film is a confessional drama in the tradition of Strindberg's *To Damascus*.[1] Like the Stranger in Strindberg's play, Isak Borg goes through the stages of a Christian confession: acknowledgment of guilt, penance, and absolution. Strindberg's conclusion is remarkably similar to the ending of *Wild Strawberries*. The Stranger enters a cloister but his conversion is not dogmatically Catholic. Rather, he commits himself to a vaguely Christian faith, based upon the concepts of love and resignation. In a similar way Isak's search explores the possibilities of love and fellowship, ending in a mellow acceptance of life. There is in much of Bergman's work a Christian ethic in which God can be completely unmentioned, and *Wild Strawberries* is a good example of this.

From a structural point of view *Wild Strawberries* carries on the Strindbergian dream play tradition which Bergman had already used in his play *The City*. The technique was described by Strindberg in the preface to his *Dream Play*:

In this *Dream Play*, as in the former play *To Damascus*, the author has sought to reproduce the disconnected but apparently logical form of a dream. Anything can happen, everything is possible and probable. Time and space do not exist. On a slight groundwork of reality, imagination spins and weaves new patterns made up of memories, experiences, unfettered fancies, absurdities, and improvisations. The characters are split, double and multiply, they evaporate, crystallize, scatter, and converge. But a single consciousness holds sway over them all—that of the dreamer.

The use of dreams as a structural device was of course not new with Strindberg, but he was the first to put on the stage a dream world in the spirit of modern psychology, and Bergman's *Wild Strawberries* is conceived in that modern vein. Non-Swedish reviewers have also suggested that the film follows up an earlier trend in the history of film-making, the cinematic expressionism of the 1920s, and that Bergman profited from the realization of older German directors: that the camera has a distinct advantage over the stage in projecting a psychic situation into symbolic imagery and in destroying the unities of time and place.

Yet, there are certain marked differences between Bergman's film and early expressionism on the stage and on the screen. Strindberg, as well as his dramatic and cinematic epigones, wrote about abstracted, nameless man. In *To Damascus*, for instance, he is called The Stranger. Other male characters in the drama—The Doctor, The Beggar, The Fool are his doubles, parts of his own psyche rather than fully rounded characters. The women—simply called The Lady and The Mother—are conceptual images representing Strindberg's various attitudes toward women.

Also in *Wild Strawberries* there is a strong tendency to depict reality through the eyes of a single consciousness, that of Isak Borg. If we adopt his point of view, the other characters in the film seem functional rather than empirical. In the dream sequences they obviously are, but in the realistic parts of the film—the journey itself—their conception is more ambivalent. People like Sara, the hitchhiker, and her two companions exist within Isak's radius. The students remind him of his youth, Sara of his sweetheart. The Alman couple has the same function as reminders, *Doppelgänger* out of the past. But as Jacques Siclier has argued, Bergman's method in presenting his main character is carried out on two levels: Isak's slow self-revelation and Bergman's examination of that revelation.[2]

The author-director's point of view is noticeable in the portrait of Agda, the housekeeper. She is an outsider in the film, against whom Isak's self-absorption is pitted and measured. In the beginning he pays no attention to Agda's wishes and treats her as a convenient but impersonal household gadget. In the end, he makes a faint overture to her feelings but is rebuffed; Agda remains an object who can help clarify Isak's development but is unmoved by it.

The role of Marianne, the daughter-in-law, is more complex and her impact upon Isak more profound. The sequence at the

house of Isak's mother shows that Marianne not only taunts Isak
into examining himself but that she experiences the coldness of his
world in a personal way. Marianne's autonomy as a character culminates in a flashback in which she reveals her marital situation.
It is the only time in the film that Bergman makes someone other
than Isak leave the immediate reality of the journey south, and it
is debatable whether this particular flashback does not destroy the
rhythm of the film, its oscillation between Isak's dream world and
the realistic contours of the journey.

How far *Wild Strawberries* actually is from literary and cinematic expressionism can perhaps be surmised by comparing it to
James Joyce's *Ulysses,* a work that holds a transitional position in
modern fiction. When Joyce, in the "Night Town" part of the
novel, penetrates to the nocturnal side of his character's mind, he
abandons the verbalizing stream-of-consciousness for a symboliz-
ing technique that seems close to Expressionism. Joyce then gives
body to Bloom's and Stephen's subconscious fears, desires, and
repressed memories. He lets these appear as apparitions and
shows deeply buried emotional complexes acted out in hallucina-
tory scenes. As Walter Sokel has pointed out, we pass from the
stream-of-consciousness, which is still a waking and, hence, a
screening process to the uninhibited outpour of the subconscious.
"But the division between external reality and inner self is never
dropped. . . . The reader knows exactly that certain associations
caused by empirical objects have given rise to the visions. In a
purely expressionistic work the framework around the vision is
dropped." [3]

In *Wild Strawberries* we have a similar situation. It is Isak
Borg's view of the old strawberry patch that leads to the most
extensive of his visions, and Bergman never lets Isak pass from the
empirical world to the subconscious without informing the spectator that Isak is falling asleep. As in Joyce, the visions are motivated by the dreamer's involvement in a given situation, and they
correspond in mood to his state of mind at the moment when he
has a dream. Thus Isak's first dream, shot in vivid black and white
in the manner of Murnau and also recalling French surrealistic
films of the late 1920s, is the most nightmarish. The setting for it
is a deserted street, a fitting commentary to the sterile landscape
of Isak's soul. Also in the next image—a man in black who, when
Isak tries to touch him, crumbles to the ground and turns out to

be a bag-of-blood man without a face—is a reflection of Isak, who is anonymous and faceless to others. The moment after this incident Isak catches sight of a hearse that comes screeching down the narrow cobblestone street and tips over like a baby carriage. A dead arm falls out of the coffin and tries to pull Isak down.[4] Peter Cowie has suggested that the wailing which attends the ejection of the coffin from the hearse "implies the proximity, almost juxtaposition of Birth and Death: the sound is exactly the same as that made later by a restless baby in a dream in which the baby seems to be a wishful projection of Isak himself; it is rocked by his sweetheart Sara."[5]

This early nightmare contains incidents which are hinted at obliquely later on. For instance, Isak sees a clock without hands, a symbol of timeless reality, of death. The image recurs about halfway through the picture, during Isak's visit to his mother, who lives in a deathlike world. The film as a whole can be seen as Isak's attempt to come to terms with the anxiety that produced the first nightmare. As he continues his inward search, Isak's fear of death subsides and his dreams become self-explorations, classical dreams that could be taken right out of Freud's *Traumdeutung:* Isak looks into the microscope of scientific knowledge but sees only himself; he diagnoses a person as dead but she is alive. Such dreams reveal his professional self-absorption and his indifference to others who are "dead" to him. Isak's last dream, finally, is a peaceful vision. Now that his conflict is about to be resolved, the images that appear to his subconscious are no more than an idyllic *Stimmungsmalerei.*

Although the tone of Isak's various dreams is easy to determine, the images which are used to convey the workings of his mind do not always seem fixed in their meaning. The spectator is invited to partake of them in much the same way as does Isak Borg himself, but what he makes of them depends upon the extent of his intellectual contemplation and personal response. It is well to remember also that Isak Borg's blindness is deep, and his road toward self-knowledge tortuous and difficult. Hence, his dreams serve both to mystify and to clarify.

Eugene Archer has suggested that some details (like the wild strawberries outside Isak's childhood home), which trigger off a dream, have the equivalent of Marcel Proust's famed *petite madeleine* that the narrator dips into a cup of tea to begin his search for *temps perdus*. Archer continues: "The essence of Proust's image, and Bergman's, is the conception that an event assumes its meaning, not from the action itself, but from the way it is regarded at different moments in time and that life is composed of a series of such isolated moments, given meaning by their temporal relationship to the *memories* of the man who experiences them." [6]

In *Wild Strawberries* all time is now, no matter whether we see scenes from Isak's youth, his mature years, or old age. To indicate this, Bergman lets Isak appear as a 78-year-old man in all the dream sequences, a technique which had been used by Alf Sjöberg in his film version of Strindberg's *Miss Julie*.

Wild Strawberries has probably the deepest literary anchoring of all of Bergman's works for the cinema, but the film is not photographed literature. Silent images, cutting, and rhythm reveal that this is a story conceived for the screen. It seems fitting that the picture was meant to serve as an act of homage to the man who plays the role of Isak Borg: Victor Sjöström, one of the creators of the Swedish cinema. [7]

CHAPTER 7

Portrait of the Artist: Mountebank or Savior?

I To Joy (Till glädje)

BERGMAN'S earliest attempt to depict the artist on the screen is *The Devil's Wanton*, in which the secondary action revolves around the writer Tomas. But Tomas' adolescent *Weltschmertz*, which isolates him from the bourgeois world around him, is only superficially related to his activities as an artist. The first more incisive rendering of the conflicts of the creative personality is to be found in Bergman's story of the musician Stig Ericsson in the film *To Joy* (1950).

The plot: During rehearsals of Beethoven's Ninth Symphony ("Hymn to Joy") at the Hälsingborg Orchestra Society, the young violinist Stig Ericsson is called to the telephone where he learns that his wife has been killed in a kerosene explosion at their country cottage. The rest of the film is a flashback telling of Stig's marriage and career. At one time he had big dreams of becoming a soloist. But his debut was a failure. In bitterness he blames his wife and deserts her. Gradually, however, he comes to accept his mediocrity and returns home. The film's final sequence brings us back to the present. Beethoven's music consoles Stig and enables him to overcome his wife's death and to accept his role as father: the film ends as his small son enters the concert hall and sits down to listen to the rehearsal.—

To reach his artistic goal Stig Ericsson was at one time willing to sacrifice his family happiness; Bergman suggests that Stig's married life began to disintegrate the moment his wife realized that to him his career was more important than marriage and family. By making Stig Ericsson a man of small talent rather than a genius, Bergman avoids the dilemma that Ibsen tried to dramatize in, for instance, *When We Dead Awaken:* the thought that a creative genius is by nature an egotist who cannot become a devoted lover without relinquishing his great artistic gift. Stig Ericsson, on the other hand, has nothing to lose but his vanity and his excessive ambition. He is seeking fame and recognition rather than outlet for his creative urge. His sacrifice of marital happiness is meaningless and, basically, without dramatic interest.

In justifying his self-absorption by means of an illusory belief in his own potential greatness, Stig Ericsson is a direct descendant of Hjalmar Ekdal in *The Wild Duck*. Ibsen understood the comical and ridiculous aspects of such a personality, but Bergman—like Arthur Miller in his version of the type, Willy Loman in *Death of a Salesman*—takes his character in dead earnest. Not satisfied with a dramatization of the mediocre artist as a blind, self-enamored failure, Bergman relegates his protagonist to the realm of tragedy and tries to have him undergo a change of heart. The task proves to be too much: instead of visualizing an inner conflict, Bergman resorts to melodrama and violent action. Sentimental incidents like the sudden death of Stig's wife and the arrival of his small son at the end become unmotivated shortcuts to Stig Ericsson's troubled psyche. In keeping with the superficial approach, the long flashback which forms the core of the film is conceived as narration rather than psychological drama; it is a reenactment of the past and not memory seen through the present.

With Stig Ericsson as his abstracted vehicle, Bergman attempts to depict three forms of joy. First, there is the precarious happiness of the artist whose joy must turn into despair whenever he fails to live up to his expectations. Secondly, there is the joy of romance and love. In the film this is illustrated most clearly in a wordless monologue on the train when Stig is returning to his wife. Echoing his early theme of happiness-in-togetherness, Bergman portrays Stig and his wife in simple scenes of fellowship: in the kitchen after a concert, at the movies, or at the seashore. Both their reconciliation and their moments of joy are set (in typical Bergman fashion) against the background of a brief summer. But the film also attempts to transcend this ephemeral happiness by suggesting a third kind of joy, expressed in Beethoven's music: the mature, solemn joy that lies beyond despair and suffering.

In its movement from youthful bliss to sudden despair and a quiet acceptance of life, *To Joy* forms a parallel to *Illicit Interlued*, where the middle-aged ballerina Mari overcomes the fixation of a young love. The main motif, the egotism of the artistic personality, is developed more fully in *Through a Glass Darkly*, the first of Bergman's so-called chamber plays.[1] In all of these films the artist succeeds in breaking his isolation, and his psychological development is, in fact, not too different from that of Isak Borg in *Wild Strawberries*. For a more complex portrait of the artist and his social function we have to turn to two of Bergman's most intriguing films: *The Naked Night* (1953) and *The Magician* (1958).

II   The Naked Night (Gycklarnas afton)

The plot: The main characters in *The Naked Night* are a circus director (Albert) and his horse-taming mistress (Anne). Like most of their fellow workers they are no great artists. But through failure, and the humiliation that follows, they reach a kind of resignation and momentary acceptance of life. Orestes' words in Sartre's *The Flies*—"Human life begins on the other side of despair" —express also Bergman's philosophy in *The Naked Night*.

The actual story concerns Albert's and Anne's experiences during a stopover in Albert's hometown. Years before, Albert left his wife (Agda) for the circus; now he is tired of being on the road and tries to effect a reconciliation with Agda, but fails. In the meantime Anne has a brief and humiliating love affair with an actor, Franz. Frustrated and enraged, Albert challenges Franz to a fight, but he is severely beaten. He plans to kill himself but does not succeed; instead he shoots a caged bear that belongs to Alma, wife of the clown Frost. In the end Circus Alberti leaves town; Albert and Anne continue their journey together.—

The fate of Albert and Anne is anticipated in the opening sequence of the film, a single flashback which tells the story of Frost and Alma. The incident takes place seven years earlier, about the time Albert Johansson decides to leave his wife. Photographed in a blinding chalky light and accompanied by incessant drumming, the sequence is among the finest that Bergman has made. The acting is mute, and the entire episode has an exaggerated, pantomimic effect, reminiscent of the jerky movement of silent films. The scene is at the seashore where Alma comes walking past a group of soldiers on target practice. The soldiers collect money to make Alma take off her clothes while a boy runs back to the circus to tell Frost. With the ironic laughter of the soldiers ringing in his ears, Frost drags Alma out of the water and carries her across the stony beach like a cross. The walk back to the circus is a Golgotha

for Frost, but the circus people cannot take him seriously—any
more than the soldiers could. They humiliate him, impelled by his
clownish appearance and by Alma's provocative behavior. Illusion
and reality are intertwined. The spectators judge by appearance
(a clown is a jester), but the artist himself is blind to reality
(Alma mistakes the soldiers' jeering for a crowd's adulation).

What Bergman's artist experiences most profoundly in his re-
lations with the outside world is a sense of humiliation. Typi-
cally enough, Albert's big dream is to reach America, where circus
people are honored by tradition. Deciding to pull an American
publicity stunt to raise his self-esteem, Albert goes to borrow some
costumes from a theater company in town. He brings Anne along
to impress the director, Mr. Sjuberg. We get a view of Sjuberg
from a Lilliputian angle: the meeting between him and the circus
people is shot from below, and Sjuberg appears enormous as he
begins to insult Albert and Anne: "We despise you because you
live in wagons and we in dirty hotel rooms; we produce art, and
you offer stunts and tricks. The plainest and least gifted of us can
spit on the best of you. Why? Because you look silly and patched,
sir, and your little lady would surely be much more fun without
her gaudy rags."

Sjuberg represents a more prestigious art form; his costumes are
more lifelike than those of the circus people and can create an
illusion of reality. Circus people, on the other hand, are easily
unmasked. Their elegance is only superficial. When Albert removes his tuxedo coat, he reveals that he has only a knitted shirt
underneath. Circus people are also more vulnerable, because they
lack the sophisticated pretentions of the people in the theater.
They are associated with the animals that share their living quarters. As Jörn Donner has remarked, the humiliation of the circus
people "is intimately bound up with the smell of sweat and stable." [2] When Albert is outwitted by the agile Franz, he is seen
rolling in sawdust, letting out the shrieks of an enraged animal.
After his defeat, Albert goes out and kills Alma's bear. His identification with the animal world is now complete; in the next scene
we see him sink down on the straw in the stable, pulling a horse's
muzzle towards him.

Not only Sjuberg and Franz, with their faked middle-class sophistication, but also Agda, representing the petty bourgeoisie, as-
sociates the circus with filth. She lives with her two boys in a small

house cluttered with Victorian bric-a-brac, and is grateful to have escaped "from that horrible circus that I always hated and was afraid of. All those shouting, dirty people, your whole world of rush and push and misery and lice and disease and I don't know what." Her present quiet life "means maturity." But Albert's reply is immediate: "To me it means emptiness." *The Naked Night* relates the settled life to the feminine and maternal: Sjuberg and Franz are both effeminate men; although Agda runs a small business, it is one of her boys that looks after the store, while Agda remains passive except when she sews on a button in Albert's coat —a mother's traditional job.

As in the opening of the film Frost again provides a running commentary on Albert's situation. In the final scene he reiterates the desire of the artist to return to a world of maternal security; he tells Albert of a dream he has had:

I dreamed that Alma came to me and said: "Poor Frost, you look tired and sad. Don't you think you need some rest?" "Yes," I replied. "Then I am going to make you as small as a foetus," she said, "and let you crawl into my stomach and there you'll have a real good sleep." I did as she told me, and snuggled down in her stomach and there I fell asleep so beautifully, so sweetly, rocked to rest as in a cradle. Then I got smaller and smaller until at last I was only a little plant seed, and then I was gone.

In Albert's case a return to the womb, i.e., to the security of Agda's world, would annihilate him as an artist. The price to pay for comfort and peace of mind is spiritual death. Albert, however, is not really free to choose: Agda does not want him; he is forced to go back to the circus and to Anne. It is upon his return that he shoots Alma's bear; in this context it is worth remembering that in Jungian studies of archetypal patterns, the killing of a bear signifies the murder of the Mother: Alma's pet animal becomes a totem of Motherhood, and its death relieves Albert of the suicidal impulses that prompted him to seek the passivity of Agda's world.

Many critics have compared *The Naked Night* to Sternberg's classical version of *The Blue Angel*, with Albert as its Professor Unrath and Anne as Lola-Lola.[3] But although the baroque style of Bergman's film is reminiscent of *The Blue Angel*, *The Naked Night* displays an entirely different set of values. When Lola-Lola tempts Professor Unrath to leave his quiet, respected position in

society, she destroys him. Anne, on the other hand, is Albert's salvation. She taunts him, but she also shares his humiliation and
loneliness; their relationship is one of mutual dependence, and in
Bergman's world this is a source of strength rather than weakness.
The conventional human community—in the film represented by
the small town—is not worth aspiring to. Bergman takes great
pains in conveying its pretentiousness (the theater) and its suffocating smugness (Agda's home). Albert's and Anne's life is tortuous and degrading. It is a life without illusions. But at least it has
integrity.

Bergman subtitles The Naked Night "a penny print on film."
The monotonous melody of a hand organ, which opens and closes
the film, and the film's external action suggest the world of popular folk literature. But the film has none of the stereotyped psychology of an original penny print. Visually it seems many-faceted
by means of mirrors and reflections, while the interplay between
character and milieu is conveyed by having the camera track a
great deal, "weaving around the sets to encircle the players." [4]
The fusion of actor and environment enables Bergman to blend
boldly a naturalistic and symbolic technique. Agda's cramped living room or the powder room in the circus where Anne is playing
solitaire are rendered with meticulously naturalistic detail. But it
is the people, absorbing as well as reflecting these rooms, that
expand the scenes from accurate milieu painting to symbolic experience. Human faces and gestures reveal and judge the surroundings. Agda's blank face reflects the emptiness both within
and around her. Albert's sweating and heaving body identifies
him with the animal life of the circus. Anne's nostrils, trembling
like those of a horse, remind us of her role of equestrienne.

The Naked Night presents the duplicity of the artist's attitude
toward his profession: loyalty and inevitable bondage on one
hand; a longing to get away, to escape into a world of security
and respectability, on the other. The film also suggests society's
view of the artist. He is a mountebank and humbug whom the
public loves to humiliate and unmask: Albert has to remove his
coat when he fights Franz; and in Agda's living room he takes off
his jacket. On both occasions he experiences defeat. Anne is undressed by Franz in his room at the theater only to find herself
ridiculed.

The theme of the humiliation of the artist is varied and amplified in *The Seventh Seal*, where Jof, the visionary juggler, is frightened out of his wits by the sadistic priest Raval as he is tortured by flames and forced to leap like a bear (one is reminded of Albert's identification with the bear in *The Naked Night*). Jof holds out his arms horizontally as if on a cross, a Christ allusion that epitomizes the artist's ambivalent position in society, his role of persecuted victim *and* divine deputy, whose rapport with the transcendental remains a secret to those who ridicule him. Jof is unaware, however, of the spell he could cast over his audience as a being with clairvoyant powers. But the film's church painter knows of his ability to frighten people: he enjoys painting realistic plague scenes in order to create an illusion of death, of the unknown; his motivation is that "it's good to scare people a little."

Albert, the humiliated circus director; Jof, the tortured juggler-buffoon; and the spellbinding church painter fuse into the composite portrait of Albert Emanuel Vogler, the "health doctor," who plays the central role in *The Magician*, possibly Bergman's most puzzling film.

III   The Magician (Ansiktet)

The plot: The film is set in early nineteenth-century Stockholm. The mesmerist Albert Vogler arrives with his party at the house of Consul Egerman, where he is to settle a bet between the Consul and a medical doctor, Vergerus, about the existence of the supernatural. Vogler remains mute before the small company, which consists of the Consul and his frustrated wife; the police chief Starbeck and wife; and Dr. Vergerus, the rationalist.

A performance takes place the following day to test whether or not Vogler has supernatural powers. Vogler begins by hypnotizing two members of his audience. In a trance Mrs. Starbeck reveals the vulgarity of her husband. After that, the coachman Antonsson is tied with the invisible chain. In fury, he tries to strangle Vogler who apparently dies. Vergerus performs an autopsy on Vogler and finds nothing remarkable about his body. He therefore concludes that the health doctor is a humbug. But the person whose body Vergerus has actually examined is an actor, Johan Spegel, whom Vogler picked up during his trip to Stockholm and who has died during the night. As Vogler's stand-in, Spegel now becomes part of a poltergeist revel in the attic, which makes Dr. Vergerus momentarily lose his mind and succumb to Vogler's magic. But safely out of the attic, Vergerus turns against Vogler and denies that he possesses any supernatural powers. Vogler, now unmasked and deeply humiliated, is about to leave the house when a message arrives that the King of Sweden desires the presence of the mesmerist and his troupe.—

The Magician opens with a scene resembling the beginning of *The Naked Night:* horses and people move forward against a darkened sky. We hear the creaking of the wagon wheels and the occasional sounds of the forest; otherwise, everything is silent. It is a gothic landscape and a fitting scenery for the mysterious Dr. Vogler and his weird-looking company. A few moments later when we move into the living room of Consul Egerman, the camera projects a realistic picture of a bourgeois house from the middle of the last century; it is a pretentious milieu but one lacking the mystical elements of the first sequence.

The house of Consul Egerman is a microcosm, a world where science, culture, and law seem to war against magic, credulity, and faith. The naive and emotional among the group are taken in by Vogler's appearance and performance, while the more sophisticated maintain a supercilious distance to the magician. Vogler's cleverness brings Vergerus to a state of hysteria; yet, once the medical doctor has calmed down, he is as condescending toward Vogler as before. After all, he says, Vogler's resurrection was merely an illusion, a trick. He performed no miracles; he was nothing but a simple charlatan. But Vogler, humiliated and defenseless, replies: "You are ungrateful, sir. Haven't I exerted myself way over my ability to give you an experience?"

In the Vogler-Vergerus relationship Bergman dramatizes the tension between the artist and a certain type of spectator who wants to deny the creative and imaginative person his *raison d'être.* From this point of view the Hitchcock-inspired attic sequence is crucial. It has been criticized as a cinematic hoax.[5] Slow, rising tension and the use of macabre props, such as loose limbs from the dissected body, have been called the cheap instruments of a sensationalist artist. But Bergman's approach is intentional; he wants to create in the audience the same feeling of unbearable suspense and fear that Dr. Vergerus experiences. Bergman seems to say to his spectators: "You may doubt me, but look, I can shake you in your aloofness and skepticism. I can make you

tremble and scream. Such is my power, and for once the humiliation is yours, for you have been taken in by my simple tricks." In a
short article Bergman has also stated that it is the privilege of the
artist to "fool" his public; for him it is permissible "to commit any
outrage, any artistic violance, tell any dizzy lies one pleases, as
long as they are truly seductive." [6] In *The Magician* it is well to be
aware of his trickery and playfulness amidst the many philosophical and religious discussions of the film.

In the final scene Vogler and his troupe depart in triumph. But
the ending is no unconditional victory for the magician. Society,
here symbolized by its formal head, the King, calls upon his serv-
ices. Yet, the invitation has its ironic explanation: it is revealed
that Aman-Manda, Vogler's assistant and wife, had earlier attracted a Grand Duke who promised to recommend the troupe to
the King.

Even so, the ending has been used to support an interpretation
of *The Magician* as a religious allegory. The King is a divine father who calls upon his son: "When the King's son, the One sent
forth, has been as deeply humiliated as is possible, there is a turn
in the tide. Then comes, says the Gnostic, the Letter, the Royal
Letter from the world outside of our reality, and conveys the
King's will: that his son shall be rehabilitated and enter into the
glory of His Father." [7]

Stig Wikander, from whose article the quotation above is taken,
draws a parallel between Bergman's film and the ancient Christian legend about the Samaritan magician Simon Magus, whose
encounter with the apostle Peter before the emperor Nero had a
progression similar to that of Vogler and the medical doctor Vergerus before police chief Starbeck, "a small-town Negro."

The religious overtones of *The Magician* are suggestive and
vague enough to support also an analysis of Vogler as a Christ
figure. Carl-Eric Nordberg has called the film "a paraphrase of the
Golgotha drama." [8] Many details seem to support such an interpretation: Vogler wears a Christ mask; he is accompanied by a
"disciple," Aman-Manda; he answers the questions asked by police chief Starbeck with the same mysterious silence as Christ before Pilate. Mrs. Egerman, who defends Vogler, plays the role of
Pilate's wife, who tried to save Christ. When Vogler is seemingly
killed by Antonsson, the police chief refers to the incident as "an

execution," while Antonsson, like Judas, goes out to hang himself. Vogler is "resurrected" and called to the King, as Christ was risen from the dead and ascended the throne of God.

Bergman's view of the artist as both a visionary and a scapegoat lends itself to religious analogies. There exists, however, an ambiguity not only in the group's response to the health doctor but also in Vogler's view of himself, a self-doubt which fits ill with his role of prophet and savior. The intensity of Vogler's self-searching, which culminates in his confession to Aman-Manda ("I hate them. . . . But I am also afraid, and then I become powerless") justifies the opinion that the basic philosophical mood of the film is one of troubled skepticism.[9]

What catapults Vogler into a questioning of himself is an early remark by Spegel: "Are you a swindler who must hide his real face?" From that moment on, Vogler does not only use his occult gift; he is also haunted by the unusual faculty he seems to have. His irritation is increased by the fact that he is under constant scrutiny, everyone in the audience desiring to penetrate behind his mask. In an interview Max von Sydow, who plays the role of Volger, has stated that Bergman had his own artist self in mind when he conceived the character.[10] In *The Magician* he depicts how he feels and reacts when he faces the threat of having his personal life dissected. The film is an answer to one Swedish critic who, frustrated by the distance he sensed between Bergman's private self and his artistic mask, sent him an open letter asking: "Have you a Face? What happened to your heart?"[11] (Literally translated, the title of the film is *The Face*.)

But the sources of *The Magician* are not only personal. At the première Bergman revealed that he had long been interested in the ideas of Mesmer and animal magnetism and for years had toyed with the thought of making a film on the subject. Several details in the picture indicate that he had studied the actual history of mesmerism in Sweden.[12]

Mesmer's theories about a universal magnetic fluid reached Sweden from Paris in 1789. Count Carl, later King Charles XIII, had mesmerism as his favorite pastime and apparently believed in it quite seriously. During the years 1815–1829 a journal was published in Sweden devoted entirely to the subject. The fad received a new impetus in 1864 when a Dane by the name of Carl Hansen came to Stockholm and put on a séance before the Swedish Medical Association, whose members were as skeptical as Dr. Vergerus in Bergman's film. Hansen failed completely in his attempt to hypnotize his audience until one of the doctors called in a servant, who easily fell under the spell of Mr. Hansen's mesmeric look.

The servant did not try to strangle the hypnotist as Antonsson does in the film, nor was Hansen called to the King's palace. Twenty years later, however, another charlatan by the name of Bishof visited Sweden and was asked to perform at the Drottningholm Palace. The result was a renewed interest in occultism. Strindberg, for instance, took part in mesmeric ceremonies and applied his experiences both in his art and his private life.

Bergman has often stated that it is the prerogative of the artist to borrow not only historical facts but also literary material. Parallels often exist between plays that Bergman has directed for the theater and the film he has been working on simultaneously. *The Magician* can in part be led back to Chesterton's drama *Magic*,[13] which Bergman produced at the Gothenburg City Theater in 1947, and where we find a decadent illusionist who expresses the ambivalent fate of the artist: to live under the power and the curse of the imagination. His situation in society oscillates, as does Vogler's, between that of an unmasked bluff and an awe-inspiring magician. Chesterton also introduces as a minor character a rationalistic doctor who argues with his sister, because she believes in miracles, and who may have inspired Bergman to draw the portrait of Dr. Vergerus.

The view that the artist's gift has magic or divine potentiality is as old as Plato, who reacted toward the poet in the same ambivalent way as Vogler's audience does toward the health doctor. Attracted to the artist, Plato nevertheless expelled him from his Republic with the motivation that his secret power endangered the stability of society. His fears would have found support in Bergman's film; Vogler's troupe creates change and chaos in the Egerman household: "Everything becomes confused, the bourgeois see themselves made ridiculous and humiliated, a dance macabre turns the established order upside down." [14]

Vogler, like Albert in *The Naked Night*, is a social outcast, a mountebank, invited and exploited by the plutocrats in order to bring a little excitement into their settled world. But Bergman,

now a successful film-maker, has begun to realize the artist's irrational hold over the minds. Thus he creates in Vogler a charlatan,
to be sure, but perhaps also a prophet,[15] a man who

> like an angry ape
> Plays such fantastic tricks before high heaven
> As make the angels weep.

CHAPTER 8

The Virgin Spring

I N *The Virgin Spring* (*Jungfrukällan,* 1960) Bergman returned once more to the world of the Middle Ages. The basis of the script was a thirteenth-century ballad titled "The Daughter of Töre in Vänge," which Bergman had read as a student at the University of Stockholm. At first he attempted to write a play on the subject; later he tried to shape the legendary material into a ballet. But when he finally decided to make a film instead, he asked Ulla Isaksson to write the script. He felt that he was unable to approach the subject matter with the stylized detachment of the balladeer.[1] What he wanted was a direct and simple rendering of the original. Ulla Isaksson, who like himself came from a religious milieu, had impressed him by her ability to recreate a historical period in her novel about witchcraft trials in Sweden, *Dit du icke vill.*

The plot: The title of Bergman's film alludes to the central event in the old ballad: the miraculous welling forth of a healing spring on the spot where a young virgin, the daughter of Töre in Vänge, has been raped and killed by three goatherds on her way to church. Like the original, the film also tells of how Töre avenges the crime by murdering the three men as they come to his farm and unwittingly try to sell the expensive clothes of the young girl (Karin) to her mother, Märeta. To atone for his guilt Töre then promises to build a church of limestone, a gigantic task in thirteenth-century Sweden.—

The student of folklore can easily show that the ballad of Töre's daughter exists in many versions, both verse and prose. Although Bergman's source of inspiration refers to an actual spring in the churchyard of Kärna parish in Östergötland, which was thought to have healing powers and around which the ballad was danced and sung, the literary prototype is to be found in the Romance languages. Not until the story reached Scandinavia, however, did it become connected with a spring of water and a church building. The Christian themes of the need for reconciliation and the certainty of God's mercy were then added to the original drama of violence and revenge. The ballad which fascinated Bergman had taken on the quality of a religious miracle play.

In filming *The Virgin Spring*, Bergman seems to have had the stylized original in mind. Ulla Isaksson, on the other hand, has above all wanted to furnish motivation for the characters: "The film must in quite another manner [than that of the ballad] make the story of young Karin and her parents realistically understandable, credible as to continuity, psychology, and milieu." [2] The result is, at times, a strange hybrid of a film, in which psychological modernisms—as for instance the Freudian approach to Märeta, Karin's mother, whose religiosity has a strong sensual quality— jars with the director's ritual conception of the story. Bergman's approach does not exclude individualized portraits of the participants in the drama, but it does not permit scenes of verbalized self-consciousness. It has been suggested that in *The Virgin Spring* the spoken word is almost completely irrelevant.[3] This is not entirely true, for although the dialogue is often stilted and over-explicit (i.e., has exactly those qualities for which reviewers have most frequently criticized Bergman's own scripts), "spoken scenes" can be made part of and even support the ritual pattern when placed in the right context. While Märeta's confession of jealousy as she and her family set out to search for Karin, whom they know to be dead, seems like an obtrusive anachronism, Töre's desperate prayer at the end of the film is quite acceptable because of its direct reference to the film's central message. Besides, the speech is such that the *realization* of the promise it contains can in part be suggested in gesture:

You see it God, you see it! The death of the innocent child and my vengeance. You permitted it. I don't understand you. I don't understand you. Still I ask you now for forgiveness—I know of no other way to *be reconciled with my own hands*. I know of no other way to live. I promise you God, here, by the dead body of my only child, I promise you that in penance for my sin *I will build you a church, I shall build it here*. Of lime and stone and *with these two hands of mine*.[4]

As Jörn Donner has observed, the speech underscores literally that Töre wants to reconcile his hands with Christianity. "He wishes to perform the penance not only of the word, but also of the deed, in order to prove his changed state of mind." [5]

The juxtaposition of good and evil, innocence and rape in the old ballad is amplified by Bergman and Ulla Isaksson to include a tension between paganism and Christianity. They present a picture of a transitional period in Scandinavia, not unlike that conveyed by Sigrid Undset in her medieval novel *Kristin Lavransdaughter*, a world in which Christianity "has not yet moved into people's understanding but . . . already involves rituals and submissions which are accepted." [6] At the same time, powerful remnants of the old heathen beliefs are still at work in the film, especially in the characters who exist outside a community of love and fellowship: in Ingeri, Karin's foster-sister who, pregnant and unmarried, is a mistrusted outcast; in the two goatherds who rape Karin; in the lonely bridge keeper who practices secret rites deep in the woods.

The portrait of Ingeri is an addition to the original. The film opens on a long, slow shot showing the dark-haired girl as she presses her belly against a post in the large manor hall at Töre's place and invokes the pagan god Odin. It is in keeping with the film's ambivalent approach that Ingeri is conceived as both a primitive folklore archetype, the evil stepsister in touch with superstition and black magic, and as a victim of sibling rivalry and social injustice. Jealous of her fair-haired foster sister, who is treated like a princess, and following a sudden impulse, Ingeri puts a toad into a large piece of bread which is to be part of Karin's food sack for her ride to church. Ingeri desires to be Karin's equal. She cannot rise; hence, she must wish Karin to fall, to be violated as she herself has been. The toad she puts into the bread is an ancient symbol of sexuality ("the toads jump in the springtime") and of evil ("When food is turned into frogs and toads, the Devil is frisking around").[7]

Accompanying Karin on her ride to church, Ingeri leaves her foster sister at the edge of the woods to enter the bridge keeper's shack. Although fearful of the old man's fey qualities, she nevertheless becomes associated with them: moments later when she flees in panic into the woods, she is so spellbound by evil wishes that she fails to intervene in the goatherds' violation of Karin, which she watches, hidden behind some bushes with a large stone in her hand. Yet, Ingeri is not the epitome of evil, for she is

haunted by guilt. In the end, she is thus prepared to receive absolution at the virgin spring.

Ingeri is indeed a contrast to Karin, who, when we first meet
her, lies in bed reveling in the memory of her success on the dance
floor the night before. Contrary to the old ballad, Karin is presented in the film as both vain and capricious. In the original she
is given the standard ballad epithet "stolts" (noble and proud),
but this as well as the enumeration of her pieces of clothing (her
skirt being "the work of fifteen young maids") serves to indicate
her privileged status rather than her vanity. Nor is there any trace
in the original of the unconscious cruelty with which Karin hurts
her mother in giving all her affection to her father or kindles Ingeri's hatred by flirting with a man who is probably the cause of
her foster sister's pregnancy.

Throughout the first half of the film, Ingeri's dark experiences
bring Karin's sexual innocence and her upper-class position into
sharper relief. The difference between the two sisters obtains
an immediate visual impact during their ride to church.[8] Karin
rides delicately sidesaddle, beautifully dressed; Ingeri in tattered
clothes slumps astride an old mare. The contrast between beauty
and ugliness is reinforced as the two girls approach the woods,
where lyrical shots of nature frame the sun-worshiping face of
Karin and are set off against the darkness that envelops Ingeri as
she enters the bridge keeper's shack. The landscape itself partakes
of the same ambiguity; it contains a magic beauty and an equally
magic evil; sweet birds caw and loathsome toads boggle in enormous close-ups. In this sylvan landscape hideous, yet Pan-like
goatherds lie in wait for the young virgin. Hungrily they invite
her to a woodland picnic, and we see "beauty and monsters side
by side, beauty too rarefied for reality, ugliness too violent for
normality." [9]

The rape and murder scene was cut in part for the release of the
film in the United States. In Sweden it created an intense debate.
The sequence has a far more immediate emotional impact than
the lines in the original ballad in which the crime is described:

> First she was three herdsmen's wife
> Then she gave up her young life.
>
> They took her by the golden lock,
> and placed her 'gainst a birchtree stock.

> They severed then her lovely head—
> A spring welled up upon that stead.

But as Bengt Idestam-Almquist (Robin Hood) has remarked, the
film could have made Karin's death even more gory, had it followed the details given in the last two stanzas above.[10] It was perhaps this part of the legend that Ulla Isaksson had in mind when
she argued that it was not possible "to reproduce with entire realism the . . . attitudes of such a distant time, and expect modern
men to understand them." [11]

Karin's death brings the first half of the film to an end. The rest
of the picture is Töre's and deals with his revenge. The camera
moves first to Töre's manor hall. The three goatherds come and
ask for lodging for the night. In the ballad they are conceived as
an abstract group; in the film they are individualized: one of them
is extremely lean and talkative; another is tongueless and inarticu-
late; the third is a teen-age boy. The aim of this characterization
was, according to Ulla Isaksson, to create pathos around the murderers and make us regard them with ambivalent feelings: "The
three criminals are not totally evil. On the whole we emphasize
that the spectators have pity for all people in this film." [12]

The goatherds are invited to share a meal with the family. Töre
presides over the supper and the entire sequence has the ceremo-
nial buildup of an altar painting of Christ's last supper. None
of the people in the household knows anything of Karin's fate. Of
the goatherds only the young boy realizes that they have come to
the home of the violated girl; he recognizes Töre's prayer as the
same that Karin had said at the meal in the woods. Remembering
the crime, the boy begins to vomit but is subdued into silence by
his older companions. Later, during the night, one of them tries
to sell Karin's cape to Märeta, who, controlling her sorrow, goes to
inform Töre. His revenge is ruthless; it is preceded by a ritual
during which he pulls down a birch sapling for his steam bath, a
scene that is almost a parody of rape although, isolated, it is beautiful in its visual richness.[13]

As the morning sun penetrates through the opening in the roof,
Töre sits at the table waiting with a slaughtering knife to kill the
murderers. His code of behavior is stark and violent: an eye for
an eye, a tooth for a tooth. Cinematically, the scene is balanced
against the rape scene: in both cases a largely static camera regis-

ters the movements of murderers and victims. In neither sequence is the spectator spared the cruel details. To make Töre's crime fully as evil as the violation of his daughter, Bergman has Töre kill also the one goatherd who is innocent, the young boy.

After the vengeance the entire household goes to find Karin. Up until then Töre has struck us as a man of primitive emotions. Now, however, he is called upon to display Christian repentance. Marianne Höök finds Töre's reaction before his daughter's ravaged body to be rather unbelievable: "Had a new fury welled up in him, or an uncontrollable sorrow, one would have been convinced. But it is psychologically preposterous that he should fall down and thank God at such a moment." [14] It is debatable, however, whether Töre is not so stylized a character as to make realistic criteria meaningless in judging him. More puzzling to the spectator is perhaps the philosophical ambiguity that Töre displays: he prays to God but doubts his goodness; he confesses his inability to understand a divine being who permits such cruelty as rape and murder, but he promises to build him a church.

The film ends with Töre's prayer and the miraculous appearance of the virgin spring (unfortunately accompanied by symbolic hymn singing). The ending constitutes Bergman's most radical departure from the original. The ballad falls into four parts: 1) Karin's preparation for the journey; 2) her rape, murder, and burial, and the miraculous appearance of a spring on the spot where her head was chopped off; 3) the arrival and murder of the three goatherds at Töre's place; 4) Töre's atonement.

It is inevitable that Bergman's transposition of the miracle to the end of the story, and placing it *after* Töre's promise to God, takes on the quality of a bargain. According to Ulla Isaksson the final scene is "Lutheran" (although it is a cornerstone in Luther's teachings that we cannot point to our deeds and ask for grace):

The final words of the film imply that we are not able, by our own power, to live our lives as human beings. The last scene when Töre kneels down and asks forgiveness, occurs because forgiveness is the only possibility. It is also of great importance that the spring wells forth when all need it. In that sense the film is very Lutheran. That this possibility exists is the very meaning of the film. [15]

But contained in the transplantation of the miracle to the end of the film lies not only a theological question but a broader, religious difference between a universe conceived in terms of total faith, and one of subtle meanings and symbolic justice. "In the film, the spring comes as a poetic apotheosis and an emblem of goodness; in the ballad it is simply there; God is not only someone who answers when called upon; he works full time." [16]

Bergman himself has indicated that the welling up of the spring was not meant as simply "the tidy expression of a religious miracle." He considered the scene a cathartic necessity: "I didn't see how it was possible to allow the picture to end without the spring, for if the father had merely gone home, and there had been a great silence, there would have been no release for the feelings of the people of the story, nor for those of the audience." [17]

In *The Virgin Spring* setting and milieu are captured with great photographic beauty and subtlety. Yet, the approach to the story is direct and simple. In crucial scenes the camera suggests no symbolic level of response. It is a recorder rather than an interpreter, and it is often quite still in a way that suggests an earlier film art. The inflexible position of the camera creates a mood of cruel spectatorship, and it is likely that the rape and murder scenes shock our sensibilities, not because of Bergman's "conscious dwelling" upon them,[18] but because his static technique pinpoints our own position as passive observers: we are locked in a visual display of horror. At the same time, however, we sense the director's distance from the subject matter. Bergman approaches the story with an objectivity and a subordination of personal feelings that he usually reserves for his stage productions. *The Virgin Spring* is, in fact, closer in cinematic style to the earlier Bergman-Isaksson film *Brink of Life* than to *The Seventh Seal*, even though the former film is set in our time and the action of the latter takes place in the Middle Ages.

CHAPTER 9

The Trilogy

BERGMAN calls *Through a Glass Darkly* (*Såsom i en spegel*), *Winter Light* (*Nattvardsgästerna*), and *The Silence* (*Tystnaden*) a film trilogy. Each work tells an independent story, but all three films are variations of a metaphysical problem that had occupied Bergman also in his earlier films: the possibilities of faith and doubt and the social and/or personal ramifications of an individual's attitude toward God. More specifically, the films explore the image of the Father in its divine as well as earthly form.

In his film trilogy Bergman moves into a world in which one detects once more the shadows of Strindberg, Kafka, and Kierkegaard. Bergman likens these films to chamber plays and compares his scripts to sheets of music. He has in mind a dramatic form which Strindberg had explored in plays like *The Ghost Sonata*, *Burnt House*, and *Storm*. But while Strindberg meant to pattern his chamber plays after the Beethoven sonata, Bergman's model is the string quartet, with special reference to Bach's music, which he also uses frequently in the trilogy. He shares, however, with Strindberg the concept of a chamber play as an intimate piece of theater, covering short spans of time and employing only a few actors; it is a dramatic work in which the emphasis is on *leitmotif* rather than conventional character conflict. The structure is that of musical counterpoint, with variations and repetitions of a theme, parallel actions, and a set of dramatis personae whose destinies are often analogous. As in Strindberg's case, Bergman's idea of a chamber play grew out of certain technical circumstances. Strindberg adapted *The Ghost Sonata, Burnt House,* and *Storm* to the small stage and allusive atmosphere of the newly founded Intimate Theater in Stockholm. In his trilogy Bergman develops a cinematic style which makes the utmost use of the camera's ability to explore the human face and reveal our innermost feelings in subtle gestures and long, penetrating shots.

Kafka's spirit, i.e., the mood of confinement and imprisonment-in-self which is now part of the *Zeitgeist* in twentieth-century art, has been present in many earlier Bergman films (e.g., *The Devil's Wanton, Three Strange Loves,* and *Wild Strawberries*) but reaches its fullest expression in the trilogy. *Through a Glass Darkly, Winter Light,* and *The Silence* depict man in relative isolation, as if he lived somewhere beyond or in the outskirts of reality. Setting and landscape—a barren island in the Baltic, an empty church in Northern Sweden, a huge but desolate hotel in a symbolic country—have the same quality of dreamlike metaphor as the strange reality that surrounds Kafka's people.

The impact from Kierkegaard is harder to determine. In a vague, philosophical sense all of Bergman's major films might be called existentialist stories. In *The Seventh Seal,* for instance, Kierkegaard's Either-Or alternative (the esthetic versus the ethical way of life) is personified in the squire Jöns who likes simple art and beautiful girls and would prefer to shun the sight of death, while the ethic personality is represented by the Knight, the man whose life becomes a search for a moral norm but who does not take the step (Kierkegaard would have said "leap") into faith. Isak Borg in *Wild Strawberries* is also an "ethical" personality, in Kierkegaard's sense, whose entire existence is questioned and whose attitude toward life must change completely in order to be meaningful. But it is only in Töre, the father in *The Virgin Spring,* that we find a person who arrives at that *credo quia absurdum* which is the last and most important stage in Kierkegaard's philosophy. Like Abraham in Kierkegaard's famous version of the biblical parable, Töre's faith is tested through the cruel sacrifice of his child (that Isak, Abraham's child, was saved from death at the last moment is irrelevant; the point is that God was capable of demanding that Isak be sacrificed, just as he allowed the virgin to be raped and killed). It is among other things this absurdist or operational faith in God and man's gradual withdrawal from it that the trilogy wants to explore. (One is not surprised to learn that Bergman had originally intended *The Virgin Spring* to be the first work in the trilogy).[1] As it turned out, *Through a Glass Darkly* was the first of the three films that have since been grouped together.

I   Through a Glass Darkly (Såsom i en spegel)

The plot: David, a middle-aged writer, has returned home after a personal crisis abroad. In a summer house on the Baltic Sea he becomes observer and participant in the drama of his two children, Karin and Minus. Karin, who is married to a medical doctor, Martin, suffers from schizophrenia and in the course of the film her condition worsens until she has hallucinations of God appearing as an enormous spider. In the end she is taken away to a mental hospital. Minus, her brother, is passing through the period of puberty and is filled with self-disgust and misogyny. His precarious state of mind throws him into an incestuous relationship with Karin. But with the help of David, Minus overcomes his adolescent anguish and his guilt feelings. The film ends on a note of rapport between father and son, and Minus experiences a budding faith in a God of love.—

Through a Glass Darkly is the first Bergman film after *Brink of Life* in which the photography is devoted almost entirely to the people. After a mood shot—a view of water reflections along the shoreline and a sweeping impression of the island in the Baltic—the camera moves in upon the four people who make up the entire cast. As they get out of the water after a swim, they display a somewhat strained gaiety, a first indication of the tensions that exist between them. Karin and Minus go to fetch the milk, and the camera oscillates between long shots of brother and sister and large close-ups of David and Martin on their way to pick up the nets. The sound pattern is adjusted to this technique: Karin's and Minus' voices are distant and fluttering, insecure as compared to the poised and ponderous way of speaking of David and Martin, who discuss Karin's illness.

These early scenes are largely expository. The first dramatic sequence is the outdoor dinner that is served in order to celebrate David's homecoming. David uses the occasion to present gifts to the others, but they are the wrong kind of gifts. We become aware of a distance between him and the others, which David helps widen further by announcing that he will soon leave again, this time to guide a cultural group through Yugoslavia. The dialogue is scanty and abrupt, and it is with visual rather than verbal means that Bergman registers the feelings that David's announcement creates: bitterness in Karin and Minus, and contempt in Martin for a person who seems his very opposite.

It is common for Bergman to gather people around a set table. The meal is a kind of ritual, a testing point in communication, where the lonely and self-absorbed are left outside. One remembers Isak Borg's dream of a childhood breakfast when he stands alone and hidden in the hallway as a spectator. In *Through a Glass Darkly* Bergman lets David interrupt the meal in order to emphasize his loneliness; the camera follows him into the house, where he breaks down sobbing. Walking up to the window he stretches out his arms, and the camera, which catches him from behind, transmits the impression of a Christ figure on the cross, an allusion to suffering that Bergman tends to use too frequently.

At the time of David's breakdown we do not know what has caused it, but gradually we learn that he suffers from guilt feelings for having ignored his family for his art. At one point he tells Karin: "When mother became ill, I went away, and left you with grandmother. I had my novel to think of. When mother died I had my first big breakthrough—I had arrived, and that meant more to me than her death." David's problem is dramatized and ironized by Karin and Minus in a short play they perform after dinner. The first act expresses the poet's temptation to give up living for fame, while the second part forms a reaction and critique of this attitude. It is one of the few scenes in the film where words and emotional message fuse, for *Through a Glass Darkly* is a work in which words (intentionally) hide more than they reveal. In attempts to establish contact, as tools to convey feelings, they are often inadequate. On a number of occasions they are even used to cover up feelings. Martin's expressed concern to David over Karin's illness has a false ring. And critics have observed that after his avowed love for Karin, Martin goes to brush his teeth as if he wanted to cleanse his mouth from a lie.[2]

After the play within the play sequence, the attention begins to focus on Karin. She has just recovered from an attack; her condition is not entirely hopeless; yet, there is no guarantee that she will ever become well.

Schizophrenia, the mental disorder which is characterized by a splitting of the personality and can lead to complete withdrawal from reality, is sometimes inherited, and Bergman hints that

Karin's mother suffered from the same illness. But *Through a Glass Darkly* is not conceived as a case study in schizophrenia. The film has, however, a rather ambiguous form with regard to its character structure. Many critics consider Karin the central character. But it is Minus who undergoes a crucial change (thanks to Karin and David), while Karin's development, her illness, has been apparent for some time although certain episodes help speed up its course. The film is somewhat reminiscent of Ibsen's *Ghosts* in which the effects of a disease are depicted with such dramatic consequence that critics and public alike long regarded the play as Oswald Alving's, while the real protagonist is Mrs. Alving. In *Through a Glass Darkly*, too, one should be careful not to confuse the most dramatic and intense part with that of a protagonist. Karin's role is to a large extent functional: her suffering leads her father and brother to a new understanding. Both David and Minus find themselves in a crisis at the beginning of the film. Minus fears the step into the unknown world of adulthood, and David has reached a point where his entire life must be reevaluated.

David's inner conflict proves a difficult task for Bergman to depict. On the basis of the idea that true compassion must grow out of analogous suffering, Bergman lets David tell of a suicide attempt earlier in the summer. Out of this experience, claims David, grew a new sense of faith in a charitable God. It is dramatically awkward, however, to have such a crucial moment in David's life narrated to us rather than visualized. Much of the incredulity that surrounds David's character stems from the element of verbalization that adheres to his crisis. (On the other hand, Bergman's technique here may be another attempt to expose the inadequacies of the spoken word.)

David's experience in the past, which should enable him to understand Karin, accentuates his failure to take responsibility for her. It is a grave negligence, for Karin has a strong need of rapport with her father. She feels more dependent upon him than upon her husband. When she is awakened in the morning by strange sounds, she goes to see David, who only has to put a blanket around her to make her fall asleep again. But the moment David leaves the room, it is as if Karin's subconscious senses his absence. She wakes up, and it is now that she makes a discovery that reveals David's detachment. In his diary there is the following note about herself: "Her illness is hopeless, but with occasional periods of lucidity. I have long surmised it, but the certainty nevertheless is almost insufferable. To my horror I discover my curiosity. The compulsion to register its course, to note precisely her gradual dissolution. To utilize her."

Later, when Karin sees God in the attic which is her hideout, it is as shocking and cruel an experience as David's disclosure in the diary. God comes toward her as an enormous spider; he is a monster who tries to penetrate her and suck her into his net, in much the same way as David's curiosity sucked nourishment from her illness.

After her attack, which is also her experiencing of God, Karin is carried away in a helicopter that descends outside the window like a veritable *deus ex machina* in the very moment when Karin sees the spider god come out of the closet. In the script Bergman makes a special point of describing the silhouette of the machine: it resembles a gigantic insect. It is not, of course, a question of whether Karin has actually seen God or has merely had a hallucination. She has experienced God in that world into which she has been driven by biological and psychological circumstances. But for the spectator it is necessary to have recourse to a non-mystical explanation of Karin's vision. The helicopter with its dark sound and fluttering, bug-like body provides the spectator with an opportunity to accept Karin's experience on purely rational grounds. But for Karin the spider god is real, in much the same way as death is real for the dying but unreal for everyone else. And it is into a realm of death that Karin goes, into total isolation. Her destiny points to the title of the film, which is taken from Paul's First Epistle to the Corinthians where he describes the moment of death: "For now we see through a glass, darkly; but then face to face: now I know in part; but then shall I know even as also I am known."

Karin's flight into the closed world of mental illness forms a parallel to David's desperate attempt at self-annihilation. In his daughter's failure to cope with reality, David recognizes his own struggle to come to terms with life. But Karin's (vicarious) suffering also frees David, so that he can, at last, reach one of his children; he communicates to Minus the message which is also that of the film: God is love and love is God.

Minus is not easily convinced, however. At first David's words are "just nonsense" to him. But suddenly he understands that a

miracle has happened; with a starry-eyed look on his face he
speaks into the camera: "Dad talked to me." Since Bergman's concept of God is related to the father figure, Minus' words could
mean "God spoke to me." And God is now a charitable God because David has shown, through his attempt to help Minus, that
he now cares for his children.

In spite of this change in David, he hardly emerges as a likeable
person, which has led some critics to interpret his conversation
with Minus as a humbug's attempt to find a new illusion for himself.[3] In the script, however, David's struggle with his own selfish-
ness is emphasized, and it seems likely that Minus' words to David
at the end of the film are to be regarded as authentic: "Your
words are terribly unreal, Dad. But I see that you mean what you
say."

Bergman has told how he began to have doubts as to the ending of *Through a Glass Darkly* when the film was being shot. He
did not change it because it is his belief that once the actual making of a film has begun, a director should not tamper with the
script, even if it happens to be his own. Instead, Bergman decided
to write a sequel to *Through a Glass Darkly*, in which the main
theme would be a refutation of David's self-protecting "security
god":

It [*Winter Light*] is a pendant to *Through a Glass Darkly*. An answer
to it. When I wrote *Through a Glass Darkly* I thought I had found a
real proof of God's existence: God is love . . . and I let the whole
thing emanate in that proof, it came to form the coda in the last movement. But it only seemed right until I started shooting the film. . . .
For that reason I smash that proof of God in the new film.[4]

II   Winter Light (Nattvardsgästerna)

The plot: The main character in *Winter Light* is a Lutheran
minister, Tomas Ericsson. The action takes place in Mittsunda
and Frostvik churches where Tomas is officiant, and covers three
hours (from noon to three P.M.) on a misty, cold winter Sunday.
The first part of the film consists of the communion service, to
which only half a dozen people have come: fisherman Persson and
his pregnant wife; Tomas' mistress Märta, who is a schoolteacher
in the small community; Algot Frövik, a cripple; the sexton Arons-
son, and an old woman. After the service fisherman Persson and

his wife come to talk to Tomas. Persson is haunted by a fear of universal annihilation through atomic war. The pastor fails to help him, and Persson later commits suicide.

The central conflict in the film, however, concerns Märta Lund-blad and Tomas. Märta is 33, nearsighted and ugly. She loves Tomas and sends him a long letter, asking him "to use her," but Tomas, a widower, claims that he cannot forget his wife. Märta learns, though, from Blom, the organist, that Tomas idealized his wife because he did not have the courage to face her deceptive nature.

Tomas once chose to take orders out of consideration for his parents. In the course of the film his faith breaks down com-pletely. In spite of this, he decides to officiate at the church in Frostvik although no one, except Märta, has come for the evening service.—

Following a musical analogy, Bergman divides *Winter Light* into three movements:[5]

1. The smashing of the coda: settling with the wishful security God.
2. Emptiness after the smashing.
3. The awakening of a new faith.

Each movement is given a specific setting: the first and the third take place indoors, in a church; the second out-of-doors, except for the quarrel scene between Thomas and Märta in the schoolhouse. Following a Bergman pattern, the psychological de-velopment within the central character is conceived as a journey: Tomas leaves the church at Mittsunda to go to the place where Jonas Persson has killed himself; then, with Märta, he continues his journey to the second church at Frostvik. The nadir of his situ-ation occurs at his discovery of Jonas' dead body and during his futile attempt to speak to Märta: a train stops their car and drowns Tomas' confession while the camera shifts angle and cen-ters on a row of ore cars whose shape is reminiscent of caskets.

At this point the spectator already knows what Tomas wants to confess. During his conversation with Jonas Persson earlier, he has refuted the "security god" of his youth, the same God that David tried to give to Minus in *Through a Glass Darkly*—a divine being who makes no great demands upon a person but who shields him from horror and fills a personal need. Tomas answers Jonas' prayer for such a god of peace and security by confessing:

My mother protected me against all evil, all ugliness, all danger. I was like a little child when I was ordained. Then everything happened at once. I became by chance a seaman's chaplain in Lisbon. This was during the Spanish civil war, and we had a front row seat. I refused to accept reality. I and my God lived in a world, a special world where everything tallied. All around us the bloody real life was in the throes of agony. But I didn't see it. I turned my eyes to my God. I believed in God. (Laughs.) An incredible, quite private, fatherly God. Who loved all men, to be sure, but me most of all.

When Tomas finally confronted this God with the cruel reality of wartime Lisbon, God changed into "a spider god." Unable to accept this, Tomas decided to cling to his fatherly God and protect Him against the outside world, in a deep feeling of possessiveness. He even went so far in his egotistical notion of God that he became jealous of Christ, because Christ also called God his Father.

Faced with Jonas Persson's despair, Tomas realizes that he stands before another Lisbon. His salvation, Bergman suggests, lies in his acceptance of Märta, who joins the group of redemptive women in Bergman's earlier films—maternal creatures whose prototype is Mary, mother of Jesus, the parent who conceives a child without loss of virginity. Mia in *The Seventh Seal*, for instance, is a medieval Mary. Her attitude toward Jof is completely maternal; her response to the crusader is that of a motherly servant. Her image returns in *Wild Strawberries*, partly in Marianne, the strong mother-to-be, and partly in Sara, the hitchhiker who makes a special point of telling Isak that she is a virgin. One may also point out that in the biblical story, Sara was Isak's mother. Turning to *Through a Glass Darkly* we find that Karin is cruelly related to the Virgin Mary in a scene where she sees herself nearly raped by God: "He came up to me, and I saw his face. It was a loathsome face. And he climbed up on me and tried to penetrate me. . . . When he could not enter into me, he quickly climbed up on my breast and my face and then on to the wall." At the same time it is Karin who redeems David and Minus.

Märta Lundblad in *Winter Light* not only suggests the Christian archetype but also embodies a critique of it. She is, as she says herself, "a guardian type person," a maternal woman, and through her profession a parent substitute. Her name may have biblical servant connotations: Märta = Martha. Some critics have also related her to the Christ figure,[6] and have pointed out that she is of the same age as Christ when he died; that she has suffered from eczema on her hands in places where stigmata occur and around her head, so that the sores formed a kind of crown of thorn; and that the Bible often depicts the relationship between God and man as a love between a man and a woman. Märta's love is, like Christ's, a love of humiliation and ridicule, and just as the Christ figure has always aroused disgust in many, Märta Lundblad often fills Tomas Ericsson with nausea until one day he blurts out: "I am sick of your nearsightedness and your fumbling hands. Your anxiety and your anxious marks of affection. You force me to occupy myself with your physical condition, your upset stomach, your eczema, your days, your frozen cheek." Yet, Tomas clings to Märta in his hour of need: sick and depressed he asks her to accompany him to Frostvik although he has earlier spurned her attentions.

But Bergman also suggests that Märta can only become Tomas' savior if she renounces an attitude of persistent servitude and meekness toward him. At their quarrel in the schoolhouse, which is a mutual unmasking, Märta says to Tomas: "Every time I have felt hatred toward you, I have made an effort to transform my hatred into pity." Märta's admission implies, in fact, that she knows she can only reach Tomas by discarding her martyr-like role.

Tomas dislikes Märta's quiet but indefatigable pursuit of him, but it is precisely her obtrusive lecturing that taunts him into a reckoning with the authoritative way of life he has known in the past, and the attitude toward religious matters that it has planted in him. Robin Wood has pointed out that one important motif in *Winter Light* is a juxtaposition of traditional beliefs and modern attitudes. Tomas is in the center of this, but the theme is also stated in such details as the opening communion scene where only the *old* woman has a natural response to the ritual and in the brief sequence in which Algot Frövik, the cripple, objects to the *electric* light in the church: it "disturbs the atmosphere of worship." [7]

Tomas' earliest dramatic confrontation with his inherited image of God as the heavenly Father occurs in his meeting with Jonas

Persson, the film's earthly father. Tomas is photographed in such a way as to emphasize his refusal to perform the role of guide and authority: "Jonas' face fills a great part of the frame, is close, strongly illuminated . . . Tomas is in the background, seems small like a child." [8] Later, by committing suicide, Jonas smashes, on a secular plane, the traditional image of the father as a strong, protective parent.

Tomas' avowed disbelief in his parents' God parallels his rejection of an obsolete view of women. In his schoolhouse confrontation with Märta, Tomas tells her: "I was brought up to regard women as higher beings, admirable beings, inviolable martyrs." Märta's task is to convince Tomas that women are real and human, not esoteric and angelic; she must make herself *present* to him (Tomas loves his wife precisely because she is absent, which enables him to go on idealizing her). To achieve this, Bergman introduces his boldest cinematic sequence so far: he lets us see Märta's face in a long, static close-up, lasting about five minutes, during which she reads a confessional letter to Tomas. By having Märta speak the letter rather than Tomas who has already received it at the time of the sequence, Bergman indicates how alive Märta has become to Tomas. Märta's performance has an intentionally embarrassing effect upon us. With Tomas we experience a sense of shame for Märta because she lacks pride, and a feeling of boredom because she iterates an old story, but also a sense of frustration since Märta seems so utterly helpless when it comes to practical matters (her awkwardness is underscored by the static camera angle). Yet, Märta also emanates a richness of feeling, a suggestion of great, unused powers; she fascinates us and repels us at the same time.

The ending when Tomas and Märta stand alone in the empty church may imply that their future relationship will improve. There is no verbal reconciliation between them, but the camera suggests "a rapport that stems from a similar attitude. Märta, photographed in profile with her head bent down, praying: 'If we could have security, so that we might show each other tenderness. If we could believe in a truth' (cut to Tomas in profile, with his head in the same position while Märta's voice continues) 'if we could believe . . .'" [9]

To many the empty church in the final scene conveys a sense of failure on Tomas' part. It seems more likely, however, that Bergman has wanted to emphasize that Tomas' new approach to God must begin on Märta's level, on a deeply personal level, beyond an ordinary Christian service. In the opening rite, the focus was as much on the communicants as on Tomas Ericsson; in the end only Tomas is in the center. One notices that in his final intonation of the words "Holy, holy, holy," Tomas' voice is hesitant; it is as if he listened to the words, and his speech stands in marked contrast to his mechanical performance of a dutiful task in the film's first sequence.

It is important also, in this context, to keep in mind Bergman's own distinction between what he calls "conviction" and "knowledge." A man's conviction is naturalistic. He is convinced that God does not exist. But he can also have a knowledge which says the opposite: that God exists. "A knowledge which is at once distinct and evasive. . . . One can cut oneself off from God and one can say yes." [10] By performing the service when he was in his legal and moral right to cancel it, Tomas Ericsson admits his willingness to "say yes."

A sequence in *Winter Light* relating to Tomas' doubts that have begun to torture him is described in the printed version as follows:

No footsteps, no closing door. No wind in crevices and gaps. *A complete silence.* [Bergman's italics.] He finds his way to the window.

No car, no trace. Not a sound, the snow falling evenly and quietly.

God's silence, Christ's distorted face, his blood over his forehead and hands, the soundless shrieks behind his exposed teeth.

God's silence.

Tomas (moaning): God, my God, why hast thou forsaken me?

This brief scene forms the nucleus of the last work in the trilogy, *The Silence* (its original title was *God's Silence*), which explores the human condition in a world that has lost touch with the divine.

III The Silence (Tystnaden)

The plot: Two sisters, Ester and Anna, travel through a foreign country, vaguely located in Central Europe. They are accompanied by Anna's young son Johan. Both sisters are in their thirties. Ester, who appears to be deathly ill, is by profession an interpreter and translator. She is unmarried and has a Lesbian affection for Anna.

Due to Ester's illness, the two sisters and Johan get off the train to stop at an old, baroque hotel. The language spoken in the country is incomprehensible to the visitors. The sight of rolling tanks and the sound of air raid alarms suggest that they are in a place threatened by war.

Ester spends most of her time in bed, while Anna meets a waiter in a nearby bar. Johan sees his mother and her lover disappear into a hotel room and reports to Ester, who goes to spy on Anna. A quarrel, filled with mutual accusations, follows between the two sisters. In the end Anna leaves the country with Johan, without being reconciled to Ester, who is left behind to die. Ester has, however, deciphered a few words of the strange language; she gives a list of them to Johan who tries to read them aloud while on the train taking him home. But the noise from the train drowns out his voice.—

A sequence in *Winter Light*, which also anticipates *The Silence*, takes place in the schoolhouse shortly before Tomas has his crucial confrontation with Märta Lundblad. One of Märta's pupils enters the room where Tomas is waiting. His older brother is preparing for his first communion and takes lessons from Tomas. Asked whether he himself is to be confirmed, the boy answers no. Besides, he adds, he is going to be an astronaut. To the boy, a representative of our space age, the church seems to be an antiquated institution. Spaceships now explore unknown worlds where God used to rule supreme.

Anna's son in *The Silence* bears the same Christian name as the boy in *Winter Light*. His journey is not a flight into space, but it is a symbolic exploration of the void that surrounds people who have lost rapport with each other and with God. At one point in the film we see Johan lie on his bed reading Lermontov's *A Hero of Our Times*, a name tag rather than an indication of his reading habits.

In the opening, expository sequence on the train Bergman leads us to identify with Johan. Arriving in the foreign city, Johan's eyes register everything: the setting sun, the row of tanks, a sleeping officer. Moments later, in the compartment Johan's glances introduce us to Ester and Anna, and throughout the film the camera often assumes his Lilliputian perspective: when Anna walks across the floor of the hotel room, her feet define the radius of vision; the old waiter in the hotel is photographed from such an angle that he reminds us of a giraffe; an electrician repairing a light fixture in the ceiling is seen from below. The child's point of view is also embodied in the group of dwarfs that live in the hotel and whom all the main characters meet in the course of the film. When Johan confronts them with his gun, they immediately enter into his world of make-believe and fall down, simulating dead. Also, the erotic scenes are related to Johan's way of absorbing reality around him. Anna's lovemaking has a certain likeness to the voluptuous picture of Rubens which her son has studied earlier in the hotel corridor. Ester's erotic self-gratification is photographed with the camera in the same position as in a previous sequence when Johan pretends that his hands are airplanes that crash. The Freudian parallel is also clear: "the masturbation scene gives associations of violation, death, shot-down dreams of fellowship." [11]

The Silence is a film without any real character development. Rather, it is an attempt at an exact expression of a mood of isolation, death, and destruction, registered and transmitted by the boy, felt and witnessed by Ester and Anna. The tension between the two women is the result of Anna's hatred of Ester and Ester's perverted love for her sister. It leads both of them to be deeply humiliated.

Anna and Ester are set up as each other's opposites, as embodiments of sensuality and intellect. Both of them lead mutilated lives and seem satisfied only when they can deny what the other possesses: language is the tool of the intellect and Anna appreciates the fact that she and her lover cannot speak to each other; Ester has a moment of peace when she can forget her body and sit down at the typewriter or try to decipher a few words in the foreign language.

Anna is preoccupied with her body; cleaning it is a ritual for her (she and Johan occupy the room next to the bath). But she also experiences the ugliness of the human body intensely. In the cabaret sequence, which precedes her meeting with the young waiter, Anna sees a man and a woman having intercourse on the other side of the aisle. Bergman emphasizes the repulsiveness of the act in both manuscript and image. Later, when Anna tells Ester of the episode, she says that she has seen a couple that "loved with each other," i.e., used each other as tools and objects. At the same time that Anna observes the lovemaking, the dwarfs appear on the stage, performing a grotesque dance; linked together they form a long, swaying tail and create the impression of an eely centipede, possibly also of an enormous phallus. Finally, Anna's own sexual experience is a nauseating coitus a tergo.

Anna lets her body, her chief weapon against the hated sister, be abused. Ester, however, is no less degraded. Her rigid self-control breaks down: she gets drunk, gives in to her sexual perversion and reveals her jealousy before Anna and her hysterical fear of death before a total stranger (the old waiter). Bergman also suggests the collapse of Ester's intellectual discipline by letting her tidy room—with the typewriter as central object—change into a messy and disorderly one, and by having the camera project pictures of her body which suggest a swollen, white insect.[12]

The sick eroticism of *The Silence* is not pornography but a metaphor for a disintegrating world; it fulfills the same function as the frequent visual references to war and chaos in the strange city, the name of which is Timoka, the dative form of an Estonian word for "executioner." What threatens the visitors to the city are the last remnants of an aggressive, masculine world, suggested by having an enormous tank fill the entire screen moments after Ester has nearly suffocated to death during one of her attacks.

In spite of the many military allusions, the authoritarian father figure is eventually "executed" in *The Silence*. Ester, the masculine woman, is left behind to die. We learn that the sisters' autocratic father (who was enormous and weighed 200 pounds) is dead. Johan's father is absent. The setting of the film is "feminine": ornamental walls, Rubens pictures, curved candlesticks, "corridors like vagina symbols."[13] Although all the characters that Johan and the two sisters encounter in the hotel are male, they are emasculated, deformed, or killed symbolically. One of the dwarfs that pass Ester in the corridor is dressed up as a bride. The bartender-lover is led and manipulated by Anna. The electrician is "shot down" by Johan. The old waiter appears as a kind but helpless fool. He frightens Johan, and in an attempt to appease the boy, he performs an obscene mime: while eating his dinner, he takes out a hot dog, arranges some lettuce around it and bites it off. Only by castrating himself symbolically can he establish contact with Johan.

With Bergman's first two films of the trilogy in mind, one is tempted to give the father figure in *The Silence* metaphysical dimensions. It has been suggested that the old waiter, who is *mute,* represents the last remnant of the divine in the modern world, an image of God as a helpless anachronism.[14] The waiter's relationship to the three main characters is illuminating. To Anna, the completely sensual person, he does not exist. To Ester, filled with a sense of abandonment, he becomes the last desperate hope, powerless himself before death but present as a need in the dying.

To Johan, the waiter is at first a kind of bogeyman, a superstitious figure who frightens him by his allusions to death and annihilation (he shows him pictures of a funeral). Later he bribes Johan with candy; together with the symbolic castration scene it can be fit into a metaphysical interpretation: the image of God as the overpowering Father changes into a modern version of Him as a benevolent Parent (one is also struck by the old waiter's fussing over Ester, like a parent attending to a sick child).

In the final analysis, however, the old waiter remains a symbolic reference but not a lasting norm. He helps Johan attain the freedom that is reflected in the boy's face at the end of the film. But he is left behind, and Johan departs holding on, not to any mementos of the old man but to a letter given him by the dying Ester. The letter, at which Anna merely shrugs her shoulder, becomes an initiation into the unknown world where Ester, Anna, and Johan have stayed, for it contains a list of words in the foreign language. The letter is also a sign that Ester has finally established contact with someone outside herself.

The feeling of desolation that surrounds Anna's and Ester's relationship is, in fact, counterbalanced by the sense of hope that emerges in their attitudes toward Johan. There is no open rivalry between them over the boy. He is important to both of them, which is not to say that Johan is unaware of a tension in his relationship with the two women. Anna hurts him by leaving him alone in the hotel; Ester bothers him by wanting to play maternal and give him affection when he does not want it. Together, however, Ester, Anna, and Johan form a kind of family. Ester is a traditional father substitute to Johan, someone who introduces him to the world of facts, who talks to him and teaches him the rudiments of a foreign language. Anna, on the other hand, is important to Johan as physical contact. She leads him into a world

of comforting sensuality: mother and son sleep naked side by side
in the huge bed; here any suggestion of adult sex is toned down
by having Johan curl up like a foetus.

It has been said that in *The Silence* words play a subordinate
role. From a purely quantitive point of view they do. But language is part of the symbolic pattern in the film. Between adults
words are weapons that destroy. Johan is aware of this; he performs a little puppet play for Ester in which he lets two mumbling
and adult-looking figures attack each other; they do not speak
clearly, "for they're afraid to." The quarrel between Ester and
Anna stresses the aggressive power of language; each sister aims
at hurting the other. If language is to be meaningful and a bridge
of contact, we have to create it anew, like a child learning a foreign tongue. Ester's first word to Johan in the unknown language
is *kasi*, Estonian for *hand*.

For the grown-ups music rather than speech forms a bond of
understanding. Ester and the old waiter communicate for the first
time when Ester's radio plays the Goldberg variations by Bach.
While we hear the music, truce exists for once between Anna and
Ester, and Johan becomes a link between the two sisters: the door
between their rooms is now open and Johan goes from one to the
other with a package of cigarettes that Ester lends Anna.

Apart from Bach and a few notes of dance music, Bergman
employs only natural sounds in *The Silence,* but these are not
used realistically. In the opening scene on the train we hear a bell,
but the train itself glides forward silently, as if in a dream landscape. In the carpeted world of the hotel, the silence is so pro-
nounced that the minutest sound—like the clinking of Anna's
bracelet—seems shattering. One understands why the film has
been called "a creative innovation in sound montage." [15]

Of the films in the trilogy, *The Silence* is the most impressive
visually. In all Bergman films it is necessary to distinguish between visual power and visual beauty. In *The Seventh Seal* and
The Virgin Spring one can speak of visual beauty. But the camera
can easily become too seductive; there is always a danger that the
spectator becomes too enthralled by individual scenes full of nature lyricism and gothic mystique, or that the cruel content attains
a poetic luster that destroys its intended purpose.

In both *Through a Glass Darkly* and *Winter Light* the landscape is ugly and barren, deromanticized like the characters. In

The Silence Bergman juxtaposes a sickening, baroque setting and the naked human face; the visual contrast is so strong that it creates an atmosphere of alienation between character and surroundings. But at no time in the entire trilogy is the landscape or milieu permitted to detract from the essential human story. It is in the ruthless yet sensitive approach of his camera to the *people* in the chamber plays that Bergman's visual power manifests itself.

In an interview Bergman once stated apropos of *Through a Glass Darkly:* "The solutions I seek are of three kinds—technical, formal and esthetic, but my goal is always to come closer and closer to the people in the story. In *Through a Glass Darkly* I found, by concentrating on only four people, a new and exciting experience and, I believe, a new direction for myself." [16] Bergman formulates here his breach with his previous works in the cinema. With the trilogy he discards the historical milieu, the psychoanalytical use of flashbacks, all technical experiments and tricks, and concentrates on conveying a visual nakedness, an asceticism that breaks through also in *The Silence* in spite of its overly decorative setting. The new approach means an even greater concentration on the human face than previously, and a cinematic form which is not built around the dialogue but proceeds from the visual. This development culminates in *The Silence,* the composition of which stresses the autonomy of each single scene, and the story emerges from separate images—realistic or symbolic—rather than from plot sequence or narrative logic. But all three chamber plays are united, not only through their metaphysical and psychological theme—the exploration and eventual death of the autocratic Father figure—but also by sharing a film style that is more bare and immediate than in Bergman's previous films.

CHAPTER 10

Persona

> Thus, if I am to be perfectly honest I experience art (not only film art) as meaningless.
>
> Preface to *Persona*

> Life's but a walking shadow, a poor player
> That struts and frets his hour upon the stage,
> And then is heard no more; it is a tale
> Told by an idiot, full of sound and fury,
> Signifying nothing.
>
> *Macbeth*

BERGMAN'S film of 1966, *Persona*, has only five characters, three of whom are marginal. The actual drama is concerned with an actress and her young nurse, with their withdrawal from life and identification with one another.

The plot: During a performance of *Electra*, the actress Elisabet Vogler has suddenly become silent and now refuses to step out of her world of self-chosen muteness. Upon her doctor's recommendation she leaves for a prolonged stay at the seashore, accompanied only by her nurse. Alma, the nurse, takes care of Elisabet in the hope of getting her to speak, but gradually she begins to play the role of patient: she reveals her private life, including an orgiastic sexual episode, while Elisabet listens in silence. One day Alma happens to read a letter from Elisabet to her doctor, in which the actress abuses Alma's confidence. Now a testing of power begins between the two women; Alma struggles against Elisabet's hold over her, but one day the separate identities of the two women dissolve and their personalities fuse. When the actress' husband comes for a visit, Alma plays the role of wife but as she speaks her words of love, she realizes how false they sound. She now believes she knows what has caused Elisabet's illness: an unwanted child. Alma gives voice to a confession that might have cured the actress, provided she had wanted to pronounce (i.e., admit) it. The film ends ambiguously, as we see, in separate sequences, Elisabet packing her suitcase and Alma leaving the summer place on a bus.—

The title of Bergman's twenty-sixth film is also the Latin word for the facial mask that an actor in the old Roman theater used to wear in order to suggest the role or type he played in a drama. Eventually, a conceptual change began to take place: *persona* came to mean the individual ("person") himself. Nowadays, *persona* has become part of the vocabulary of modern psychology; in Jungian terminology it means the mask we wear in public, the role imposed upon us by society. A complete abandonment of our *persona* would, according to Jung, lead to a state of mute unconsciousness; a human being would stand face to face with his naked self (and with the absolute).

Bergman's film may be related both to the original and latter-day usage of *persona*. Elisabet Vogler's silence is not simply a mental aberration; her doctor rules out the possibility of a "hysterical reaction." At the same time, however, the doctor looks upon Elisabet's muteness as a form of play-acting and advises her patient to remain that way "until you find it uninteresting, finished, and can leave it as you have left, by and by, your other roles." This advice does not prevent the doctor from realizing that Elisabet Vogler's decision is also a result of "the hopeless dream about being. Not seeming, but being. The feeling of dizziness and the perpetual hunger for unmasking. To be looked through, reduced, perhaps wiped out. Every accent a lie and a treachery. Every gesture, a falsification."

Elisabet Vogler's withdrawal is an admirable search for integrity as long as no one else is involved. But Bergman relates it to the outside world where it must be judged an irresponsible and egotistical act. Elisabet Vogler has a child whom she neglects: motherhood is a *role* she has discarded.[1] According to the confession that Alma pronounces as a stand-in at the end of the film, Elisabet became pregnant in order to prove that she could "play" the part of mother. But as her pregnancy progressed, she became nauseated by it and wanted to escape from it. She tried to do away with the child (as she has thrown off her mask as Electra), but in vain. She then grew to hate the boy. Early in the film we see her tear up a picture of him; Alma's forceful attempt to draw Elisabet out of her closed world (i.e., recognize her child as real) occurs only after she has found the actress attempting to hide with her hands the torn pieces of the photograph.

By that time Elisabet Vogler has traveled a long distance, from partial to complete withdrawal and back (perhaps) to a world of response and commitment to others. Alma, victim *and* instrument, represents the outside world, but other manifestations of life sieve into Elisabet Vogler's isolated existence and "tease" her, to quote the doctor. Some of them can be dismissed as false or pretentious: a letter from her husband is torn up, a voice on the radio is shut off. Others frighten her because they are hateful and destructive, suggestions of death and therefore genuine. When Alma threatens her with a pot of boiling water, Elisabet cries out in fear. Watching on TV a Buddhist monk in Vietnam burn himself to death makes her withdraw to one corner of the room, horrified and screaming.

Elisabet is shocked by the monk's incineration because she recognizes in it a conscious act of self-destruction, a more consequential protest against life than her own withdrawal. Her compromise is commented upon ironically by the doctor who, during a visit to Elisabet's hospital room, says: "Kill oneself? No—that's too horrible, one doesn't do that."

Life in the isolated beach cottage in which Elisabet and Alma spend the summer, is a world without contact with the outside; there is no radio or TV set in the house and no printed newspaper. Elisabet's withdrawal is complete. A brief sequence, which might be compared to the Vietnam episode, telescopes her alienation: she lies on her bed in the summer house, studying with perfect calm the photograph of a Jewish child in front of Nazi guns in the Warsaw ghetto. The episode, which anticipates the revelation of Elisabet's lack of love for her own boy, arouses no visible reaction in her. By this time, too, she has begun to look upon Alma's confessions as an interesting performance, even though at times she approaches the nurse to "caress her like a sister."

In the book version of *Persona*, Elisabet's self-absorption is stated more explicitly than in the motion picture. Her letter to the doctor emphasizes her sense of well-being at dwelling in a placid, elemental world, one reminiscent of the clown Frost's dream in *The Naked Night:* "I begin to retrieve . . . an avid hunger before dinner, a childish sleepiness at night, the curiosity about a fat

spider, the pleasure of going barefoot. . . . I feel a new health, a
barbaric frolic, I am surrounded by the sea and I rock like a foetus
in the womb." In the primordial coastal landscape Bergman can
offer Elisabet an alternative to the monk's suicide: a kind of re-
birth. For her reactions are, in a sense, those of a newborn child;
her awakened hunger for life is primitive and egotistical like a
craving baby's.

Elisabet continues to thrive largely because of Alma's self-
surrender. She feeds upon her nurse's confessions, as she admits in
her letter: ". . . she [Alma] tells me big matters and small ones
about herself. As you hear, *I stuff myself* on everything I can get
hold of." [2] The image of Elisabet Vogler as a kind of vampire is
rendered directly in a later sequence where Alma slits her vein
and Elisabet avidly sucks her blood. That this theme is essential in
Persona seems corroborated by the fact that an early name for the
film was *The Cannibals*.

The film is not a personal document, but there appears to be a
definite analogy between the fate of Elisabet and Bergman's own
statements about himself in the preface to the printed version of
Persona, which was originally an essay written in 1965 when
Bergman was to receive the Erasmus Prize in Amsterdam. Bergman relates how he, as a child and youngster, tried to impress
others with his talent; when he failed to do so, he withdrew into
himself but later discovered the futility of such a life; he wished to
communicate with the outside world. At the same time, however,
he had become aware of the useless function of art in a world
where most people's lives are full of potential drama. But he continued to create, and he will continue to make films, driven to it
by an insatiable "curiosity," a kind of hunger: "I make notes, I
observe, look, all is unreal, fantastic, frightening or ridiculous. I
capture a flying speck of dust, maybe it is a film. . . . I circulate
with my own captured object and am occupied in a happy or
melancholy way." Bergman also stresses the fact that the artist is
"free, shameless, irresponsible." [3]

Persona could prove a treasure hunt for those who know Bergman's earlier production, for the film is shot through with references to past Bergman works. We see a slapstick sequence from
The Devil's Wanton. The name of Alma was also used for
Frost's wife in *The Naked Night*, another woman "exhibition-
ist," and Vogler was the name of the health doctor and artist

in *The Magician*. The young boy from *The Silence* appears again, reading the same book, etc. Many themes recur, especially from the films about art and artists: the ridicule of the feigned world of the theater ("an old beloved lady who has seen better days"), projected by a shot of Elisabet Vogler's face in a grotesque Electra mask, echoes the criticism of the theater company in *The Naked Night*. The artist's role as therapist—a view suggested by Alma early in *Persona*, to which she also succumbs—had its aspect of derision in *The Magician*. And the conception of the creative personality as a self-centered usurper of life around him stands in direct relation to the image of David, the father in *Through a Glass Darkly*, just as both Alma and Karin (David's daughter) learn through written notes that they have been exploited.

But *Persona* is more than a crossword puzzle in Bergmaniana. True, in Alma, the nurse, and Elisabet Vogler, the actress, Bergman has polarized his favorite motifs: the maternal, "caring" aspect of the human psyche versus the masculine, life-denying; the role of the sacrificial victim versus that of the redeemed person; the exploited object facing the artist-manipulator; the seeker of God meeting an ambiguous image of attraction and negation. The metaphysical implications of *Persona* have been the point of departure for several discussions of the film.[4] The image of God finds its psychological correlative in the naked but mysterious self of Elisabet Vogler. She is a being with "severe eyes," according to Alma; she is treacherous, detached and yet at times kind and patient; she allures and repels at the same time. She is half benevolence, half "spider-god."

The metaphysical perspective of *Persona* seems to me, however, of minor importance; while a film like *Winter Light* cannot be meaningful without a religious frame of reference, *Persona* does not benefit much from an "allegorized" interpretation. But there is certainly in the film an expressed need for a belief of some kind, for a definite and stable point of reference, within which the individual can function. Thus Alma tells Elisabet:

At the hospital where I got my education, there is an old people's home for aged nurses. For people who have been nurses all their lives and have only lived for their work. Who have always worn a uniform. They live there in the small rooms and die in the vicinity of their hospital.

. . . To believe in something so strongly that you devote your whole life to it. . . . To have something to believe in. To do something, to feel that your life has a meaning. That's what I like.

These older colleagues of Alma "have always worn a uniform"; they have become one with the role they have chosen in life. Alma, by contrast, doubts that she is capable of such dedication, and during her stay with Elisabet Vogler she becomes more and more disoriented about herself instead of attaining a sense of completeness that should come from absolute devotion to a task. What prevents her from merging with her nursing role (and saves her from becoming a mere symbol in Bergman's scheme of values) is a certain *amour propre*, a growing awareness of herself as a physical being. She dwells upon her sexual experiences; she begins to study her face and discovers a physical resemblance between herself and the actress. Bergman suggests the self-absorption of such an attitude by having Alma and Elisabet wear large shielding sun hats (with biting irony these have the shape of the straw hats worn by Vietnamese farm laborers[5]); Alma also makes a point of telling Elisabet that she has worn a similar head-gear during her orgiastic sex experience.

Amour propre also dictates Alma's conversion of her admiration for Elisabet Vogler into wishful identification. Yet, the gradual realization that one identity can merge with another is a shock to Alma. Having revealed her secrets to Elisabet, she bursts out crying: "It doesn't make sense, nothing hangs together if one starts to think about it. . . . Is it possible to be different people right next to each other, at the same time?" The question receives an answer at the critical moment in the film: sitting opposite the mute actress Alma repeats twice the story of Elisabet's failure to play the role of mother. In the first sequence the camera angle is in line with Alma's view of Elisabet, but in the second sequence it has changed to the spectator's view of the two women. We see Elisabet from behind and Alma's face is now in focus; as she pronounces the confession the second time, her confusion increases until her identification with Elisabet seems complete. The face we see, finally, is half Alma's, half Elisabet's.

Bergman's skepticism toward language has always been great. In *Persona* words only exist in the form of monologues and letters.

Such linguistic asceticism seems a further development of the handling of language in the chamber play trilogy. Suggestions of the insufficiency and ungenuineness of language were present already in *Through a Glass Darkly*. The author-father David wrote a stilted prose that nauseated him. In one sequence we saw him labor over a long sentence, which he polished word for word until only the essential remained. Such a process of reduction continued in *The Silence* where the words spoken by the population in Timoka were hardly more than gibberish to the main characters, while understandable language was, to a large extent, a destructive tool. In *Persona* a friendship appears to exist between the two women until Elisabet makes use of language in the form of her letter to the doctor.

The enigmatic and largely silent world of Timoka is in *Persona* reduced to the character of Elisabet Vogler. It becomes the task of Alma to give language, and the reality outside the self (her monologues are possible only because she has a *listener*) a justification. As she is being drawn into Elisabet's closed world, she tries in a desperate moment to force Elisabet to speak to her. But on the critical occasion when her identity merges with Elisabet's, Alma's speech dissolves into pieces and she can only utter a series of disconnected words. Afterward, when she has put on her nurse's uniform again, she can no longer entertain her patient with would-be wise confessions. She has looked into Elisabet's abysmal world and all she can tell her patient is one word: nothing. But it is a word that covers Elisabet Vogler's reality and she answers Alma like an echo.

The process of linguistic reduction in *Persona* has its counterpart in the ascetic and barren milieu in which the characters move. The rooms in which they stay have hardly any furniture; the walls are naked, the light pale and economical. The landscape outside the summer house is a rocky stretch of coast on the Baltic. Bergman returns in *Persona* to the locale of *Through a Glass Darkly*; it is a marked departure from the decadent and turgid milieu of *The Silence*.

Persona has no definite ending. The final sequences when the two women apparently go their separate ways are open to many interpretations. Bergman gives no definite answer; he merely lets the film come to an end—only one in many instances in the film when Bergman destroys the illusion for the spectator. Again and again in *Persona* we are made aware of film as a constructed, "artificial" medium: the film strip jumps out of the projector; pieces of unused celluloid flicker past our eyes; the frame shows a curtain very much like that in a motion picture theater; Elisabet Vogler steps forward quite impudently with a camera in her hand to photograph *us* instead of Alma and the landscape. Thus, we are forced to realize that the story is merely a piece of fiction; that what we witness is only a film strip, "an awfully precise march of twenty-four frames per second." [6] It is hardly surprising that an early title for *Persona* was *Film*.

But *Persona* is not merely an experiment in the art of cinematography (a favorite word of Bergman's). The film also conveys a desire to stimulate the viewer. The opening sequence may serve as a case in point. *Persona* begins with a series, or rather an agglomeration, of swift images: a sacrificial lamb, a hairy spider, a nail driven into a hand, a mutilated child, etc. Almost all of the images are taken from, or have some reference to, Bergman's earlier films. But now he presents them to us in an absurd, technical way as if he wanted to tell us that they were, after all, just magic tricks. Yet, it is just as likely that Bergman has wanted to put the spectator in a receptive mood and wake him emotionally, much the same as the Spanish film-maker Buñuel did in his now classic film *The Andalusian Dog*.[7] *Persona* demonstrates, in fact, what the writers of the so-called new novel have set forth in their program: that art can be an interplay between creator and receiver; that its function is not to soothe or entertain but to activate. Alma says at one point relatively early in the film that she believes people need the artist as a therapist, that art can help many, especially "those who suffer." Her remark is meant to be ironic. Bergman questions the cathartic function of art in our time. The artist is no healer; he exists for his own sake only. Yet, Bergman also suggests (in the preface to *Persona*) that it is his hope that, once the film is over, "the shadows" shall live on in our retinas and in the most sensitive nerves of our ears.

The ultimate irony of *Persona* is perhaps that Bergman proves himself to be such a skillful artist that he draws us into the world of the film at the same time that he allows us to free ourselves from its magic, just as Alma is first sucked into Elisabet's world but at the end is apparently (she dons her uniform again) freed from its influence. We leave the theater, after having seen *Persona*, realizing not that art is a substitute for life or a refuge from it, but that art and life coexist. Bergman may believe that art is without value to modern man; but *Persona* seems to prove the opposite.

CHAPTER 11

The Comedies

"This [making a comedy] is the most amusing
thing that has happened to me since I learned
to ride the bicycle."

FOUR of Bergman's films to date—*A Lesson in Love* (*En lektion i kärlek,* 1954); *Smiles of a Summer Night* (*Sommarnattens leende,* 1955); *The Devil's Eye* (*Djävulens öga,* 1960); and
All These Women (*För att inte tala om alla dessa kvinnor,* 1964)
—are predominantly light and humorous in style. They have often
reminded foreign critics of the comedies of Ernst Lubitsch, but
actually the elegant eroticism characteristic of both Lubitsch and
Bergman finds its source in the works of the Swedish motion picture director Mauritz Stiller. His frivolous comedy of marriage,
Eroticon, made in 1920, is the prototype of the so-called Lubitsch Touch: "the treatment of adultery not as a tragic theme but
as the basis for a witty exposition of human foibles; the mood of
sensuous luxury in costumes and manners; and the insinuating,
sexy dialog." [1] In Bergman's case one can also sense an impact
from a literary predecessor; in his comedies the (Strindbergian)
love-hatred of his darker films is transformed into an ironic and
disillusioned knowledge of human nature that bears distinct resemblance to the tragi-comic novels and plays of Hjalmar Bergman.

The first time we notice an element of sophisticated eroticism in
a Bergman film is in the final elevator incident in *Secrets of
Women,* which proved to be the film's most memorable scene.
Bergman was excited at the thought that he could *amuse* the public. It is also possible that Bergman got the idea of making a full-
length comedy when he saw the professional rapport between
Gunnar Björnstrand and Eva Dahlbeck in that film. At any rate,

in *A Lesson in Love*, these two actors play the leading parts, the gynecologist David Erneman and his wife, Marianne.

I   A Lesson in Love (En lektion i kärlek)

The plot: Like the married couples in *Secrets of Women*, David and Marianne Erneman are approaching middle age. Sixteen years of marriage have produced two children and a certain amount of ennui. David tries to escape the tedium of married life by having an affair with a patient, Suzanne. Marianne responds to her husband's erotic escapades by rushing off to Copenhagen, where she meets a former fiancé, a rather boorish sculptor. The film ends on a conventional note of reconciliation: husband and wife break off their extramarital liaisons, and withdraw to the bedroom of a Copenhagen hotel, assisted by Cupid himself who hangs the sign "Do not disturb" on their door.—

The main theme of *A Lesson in Love* echoes the central motif in *Secrets of Women:* a woman has to learn to accept a man's inadequacies as lover and husband. But Marianne Erneman is neither embittered nor resigned. She displays a controlled passion, which serves as an erotic stimulant to her husband. Through a combination of cool surveillance of the marital situation and a somewhat maternal humoring of David, she emerges as the victor.

In a sophisticated erotic relationship there is almost always, according to Bergman, an element of gambling. *A Lesson in Love* has a narrative frame which revolves around a bet made by two men about a woman with whom they share a compartment in a train and whom each attempts to make his booty. But in the end the winner, who is David, is outwitted by the object of his virile attack: the woman turns out to be Marianne.

The mood of erotic caprice that surrounds the bet characterizes that part of the action which takes place in the present. But Bergman's comedies have often somber or nostalgic overtones. *A Lesson in Love* changes tone in the four flashbacks that aim to give us further insight into the main characters. In the most interesting of these glimpses into the past, David meets his tomboy daughter Nix. Feelings of distrust and childish defiance characterize the girl, but her bitterness is ironically mollified when David offers her cocoa and whipped cream, the same treat that the old Consul gave young Doris in *Dreams*.

Nix is a disillusioned child but her attitude is not only a questioning of an older generation but of life itself. She has the need of the young to live forever and is frightened by the thought of death. But it is in keeping with the predominantly light tone of the film that she finds a consoling answer; her grandfather tells her: "Death is only a little part of life. Think how dreary it would be if everything were the same, always, always. Therefore there is death, so that there may come new life for all eternity. Think only how tiresome it would be for me to wear long underdrawers a hundred thousand years."

This answer—death as a release from boredom—is skilfully made part of the mood of the film. The overriding question for its characters is what to do about life; not because it is tragic or meaningless, but because it is so tedious; even Nix admits that part of her problem is that all her girl friends seem such bores to her with their silly affectations and erotic chatter.

While *A Lesson in Love* became Ingmar Bergman's first economic success at home, it was his second comedy, *Smiles of a Summer Night* that led to his international breakthrough.

II   Smiles of a Summer Night
(Sommarnattens leende)

The plot: The film tells of the humiliation of Fredrik Egerman, a lawyer who is married to a girl twenty years his junior. From an earlier marriage he has a grown-up son, Henrik, who is studying for the priesthood.

After watching a performance at the local theater, Fredrik Egerman looks up his former mistress, Desirée Armfeldt. His visit leads to his gradual loss of dignity: first he falls into a puddle of water and has to change clothes. Desirée hands him the nightshirt of her current lover, Count Malcolm. Dressed in this ridiculous attire, Fredrik Egerman is taunted by Desirée, who mortifies him by refusing to acknowledge that her child is fathered by Fredrik. Finally Egerman is confronted with his rival, who appears dressed in full military attire.

The central sequence of *Smiles of a Summer Night* takes place in and outside the castle of Mrs. Armfeldt, Desirée's mother. Here we witness the three smiles (or "loves") of the summer night, commented on by Petra, the maid, and Frid, the groom. The first smile, occurring between midnight and daybreak, is the smile of young and pure love: Anne, the virgin wife, elopes with Henrik, the student of theology. Just before dawn the summer night reveals its second smile, "for the clowns, the fools, the unredeemable", when Count Malcolm and his wife are reconciled to each other on their own terms:

CHARLOTTE: Swear to be faithful to me for at least—
MALCOLM: I'll be faithful to you for at least seven eternities of pleasure, eighteen false smiles and fifty-seven loving whispers without meaning. I'll be faithful to you until the last big yawn separates us.

Finally, as the sun rises over the fields, the summer night puts on its third and last smile for "the sad, the depressed, the sleepless, the confused, the frightened, the lonely." The smile is for Fredrik Egerman.—

It is part of Bergman's skill that he can let Egerman become humiliated by everyone and yet have him emerge not as a mere clown but as a lonely and sympathetic man. The crucial scene in this context is the elopement. It is composed so that Egerman is all the time present in the gray distance, watching and making feeble motions to interfere. After the carriage with Anne and Henrik has disappeared "as if in a dream," Egerman goes to pick up Anne's white veil, which has blown off and lies on the ground. One critic has blamed Bergman for banal symbolism—the loss of virginity[2]—but the scene is not a pictorial metaphor for a maiden's loss of innocence so much as an image of Fredrik Egerman's shattered hopes. Standing there with the bridal veil in his hands he is stricken by the painful truth (but one that he has suspected all along) that he was too old to possess physically his young wife.

The action of *Smiles of a Summer Night* takes place in 1901. In contrast to his later historical films, such as *The Seventh Seal* and *The Magician,* Bergman is not using the past as a foil for the present. He merely recreates a bygone social situation, dramatizing the roles played by men and women in a world which is still a bourgeois patriarchy. But male authority is only an illusion. It is the women who have the upper hand in the erotic battles, while the men are usually ridiculed. The women are anchored in their traditional roles as wives and mothers, even when they are professional women like Desirée Armfeldt. The men, on the other hand, are split in their desires; they move between three worlds without feeling at home in any: the world of work, of home life, and of free eroticism.

Although *Smiles of a Summer Night* repeats the erotic constellations from other Bergman works, the immediate source of inspiration is *The Merry Widow*, Lehar's operetta, which Bergman directed at the Malmö City Theater in 1954. *Smiles of a Summer Night* is constructed as a game of musical chairs and follows the same pattern as the Vienna musical. Thus we find the standard four couples of the traditional operetta: the tragic couple, the comic couple, the romantic couple, the commenting couple. Bergman has mentioned the conventional structure of *Smiles of a Summer Night* in an interview: "*Smiles of a Summer Night* does not pretend to be more than a momentary entertainment, a playing with all the clichés of the comedy of manners; the old castle, the young lovers, the duel, the elopement." [3]

As a film critic pointed out after the première of *Smiles of a Summer Night* in London, the pattern of the comedy of manners "allows Bergman to achieve some brilliant transitions and interplay between lyricism, farce, fantasy, satire and naturalism, and keep the whole incredible confection under control." [4] It may have been a lack of understanding for the theatrical background of the film (and for the fun that Bergman was having with the old operetta style) that led an American reviewer to comment: "It [*Smiles of a Summer Night*] would have been a masterpiece of sophisticated humor had the sophistication not been interspersed with vaudeville situations." [5]

Smiles of a Summer Night employs a rather conventional dramatic structure in that the theme develops in psychological progression and not in flashbacks as in many earlier Bergman films. Fredrik Egerman's visit to Desirée in the theater ends what more or less corresponds to the first act in a traditional drama, i.e., the exposition and rendezvous of the dramatis personae. The key sequence in the second half of the film, which is analogous to Act II in a theater play (the elucidation of the theme), is shot in the large dining room of old Mrs. Armfeldt. Much of its impact upon the spectator is due to the exquisite setting. An enormous chandelier hangs from the ceiling; the long table is arranged so that Mrs. Armfeldt resides alone like a mater familias on one side of it, and the six guests are seated in a row on the other side. The sound track catches the clinking of glasses, and the camera moves in and

away from the characters in a manner suggesting the rhythm of a
dance or a ritual.[6] Old Mrs. Armfeldt is synonymous with the
film's basic attitude of frivolity and gallantry; she guides the erotic
play of the three couples like an old libertine. She lives a comfort-
able life based not upon lies but upon the suppression of truth
(her estate is hers as a gift against her promise *not* to write her
memoirs). But old Mrs. Armfeldt also realizes the futility of trying
to hide the truth. Lying in bed she tells Desirée: "One can never
protect a single person from a single suffering. That is what makes
one so terribly tired." It is a statement that sums up the philosophical direction of the film.

Young lovers appear in a great number of Bergman's films. In
his early production they are presented as victims of a hard and
cynical world; in the works from his middle period they are often
an idealistic norm (Jof and Mia in *The Seventh Seal;* Anne and
Henrik in *Smiles of a Summer Night*); in a relatively late film,
such as *The Devil's Eye*, they are mildly satirized.

The mature man who engages in an erotic game is portrayed as
a likeable but pathetic fool even if—as in *The Devil's Eye*—he
happens to be Don Juan himself. In his third comedy Bergman
returns to the well-known constellation from *Dreams* (the Consul
and young Doris) and *Smiles of a Summer Night* (Egerman and
Anne): a man of experience fails to win the heart of an innocent
girl. This time the game is viewed *sub specie æternitatis*.

III   The Devil's Eye (Djävulens öga)

The plot: Don Juan has spent three hundred years in Hell
when the head of "this inverted parish" gets a sty in his eye. The
reason is that a twenty-year-old girl wanders about on earth with
her maidenhead still intact. Don Juan is ordered to return to the
earthly paradise, bringing with him his lusty and humorous servant
Pablo. Like some half-cynical version of Cervantes' picaresque
couple, Don Juan and Pablo set out not to defend a young lady
but to rob her of her virtue. While Pablo indulges in an erotic
escapade with the girl's mother, the wife of a minister, Don Juan
concentrates on the young girl. But he falls in love with her,
which means a defeat for the evil powers of Hell. Pablo too fails
in his mission, for his brief affair with the vicar's wife merely
brings her closer to her husband. However, the devil learns later
that the young girl lies to her husband on their wedding night.

This is, after all, a small victory for Satan and the sty in his eye disappears.—

The touch is lighter in *The Devil's Eye* than in Bergman's earlier comedies. Bergman considered the film "a sort of joke," [7] and subtitled it "a rondo capriccioso." The musical reference is demonstrated at the opening of the film by Scarlatti's courtly and slightly demonic music.[8]

Bergman has acknowledged a possible influence from the "Don Juan in Hell" episode in Shaw's *Man and Superman,* which had been performed in Sweden not long before Bergman began to work on *The Devil's Eye.* But Dante's *Divine Comedy* may also have lent him some details. Thus Bergman compares Hell to a cone with a strictly hierarchical construction, an image suggesting Dante's Hell, which was likened to a funnel in the ground. In both Dante's and Bergman's versions, the Devil sits at the bottom of the cone or funnel. But there the analogy ends; Bergman's Satan is no medieval monster, locked in burning ice; he is a sophisticated, wily creature, speaking in *sotto voce* and fawning a respectable front. Instead, it is Don Juan who displays some of the defiant and rebellious features which are conventionally associated with the devil: "I remain Don Juan, despiser of God and Satan," he pronounces haughtily at the end of the film.

The Devil's Eye is possibly the most theatrical of Bergman's films. It is divided into three acts, each one introduced by an actor, dressed in black and with a shooting script in hand. The technique may be said to be analogous to the use of a historical setting—his objective correlative—in several other Bergman films. It not only helps to create a distance between Ingmar Bergman and the material at hand; it effectively foils any attempt on the spectator's part to become involved in the story. In a comedy such a *Verfremdungs-technique* allows the spectator to laugh at his own follies as these are reflected in the characters on the screen.

Theatrical features in *The Devil's Eye* are also found in the design and movement of the film, in the dramatic exits and entrances of the characters. No other Bergman film is so static in its camera work. But again Bergman transcends the limitations of a theatrically conceived film by frequent close-ups.

In a pamphlet published before the Swedish première of *The Devil's Eye* Bergman said, addressing himself to his "dear, frightening public": "Sometimes I feel as if I were already dead, stuffed and incorporated into the film-historical archives. . . . Playfulness is my weapon against the unreality of fame. So for me playfulness is necessary." [9] The statement could stand as a motto for Bergman's last comedy to date: *All These Women*.

IV   All these Women
(För att inte tala om alla dessa kvinnor)

The plot: Felix, a virtuoso cellist just deceased, is lying in state, while his "widows" (his wife and mistresses) pass by the bier. The critic Cornelius is also paying homage to the master by putting the manuscript of his biography of Felix upon the dead man's body.

A flashback brings us back in time a few days. Cornelius is visiting Felix to obtain information for the last chapter of the biography which is to reveal the innermost realm of the personal. He is not very successful but finds consolation in the rich material offered him by the various women that fill the house. In return for the confidence of Felix's wife, Cornelius reveals that he has dedicated a composition to Felix, entitled *Song of the Fish* or *Abstraction No. 14*, which he hopes will be performed by Felix.

Next, Cornelius meets Bumble-Bee, Felix's favorite mistress, and performs a striptease with her which, however, is cut short in order not to offend the censors. When he wakes up the following morning in Bumble-Bee's bed, Cornelius is nearly killed by a mysterious woman in black, who thinks he is Felix.

Cornelius' attempts to get to see Felix are all in vain. He is quite offended by Felix's inaccessibility, for he believes he is a greater genius than Felix, the artist; and besides, he "knows" that an artist "who never had his biography written will be forgotten."

In the final sequence we are back at the bier. Cornelius is trying to read out loud from his biography but discovers that the most important chapter—about "the essence of the personal"—is gone. At that moment a young cellist walks in, and as he begins to play all the women know that a new master has arrived. Felix is not only dead, he is forgotten.—

The film is hardly subtle in its approach; the transparent satire is directed against the biographical school of criticism, which has always had a stronghold in Sweden, and against reviewers who have never tired of telling Bergman how to make a film. Bergman speaks up for the integrity of the artist, using the statement by one of the women in the film as his guiding principle: "It is the playing that counts." (Peeved critics suggested that Bergman was merely finding excuses for his notorious unwillingness to meet the press.)

As a piece of cinematic art *All These Women* has very little to offer, even though the technique is less theatrical than in Bergman's previous comedies and though his first attempt at color is interesting—a contrapuntal element used to emphasize the mood, all the way from somber shades in the tragicomic episodes to gay nuances in the farcical incidents. But the film suffers from an episodic structure, which leaves less to the actors and too much to the dramatic action. The dialogue has little of the sophisticated wit of the earlier comedies; it is strained and at times merely crude. On the other hand, the cutting tone is in keeping with the aim of the film: to make fun, not only of the critics, but of censorship, of visual and verbal artificiality, of conventional humor. The plot is intentionally banal and filled with slapstick and gags of the simplest kind (hero falling into a pond; hero dressing up as a woman; hero lighting fireworks by mistake). Such features are acceptable only if one constantly keeps in mind that *All These Women* is designed as film-as-extended-caricature. But making fun of cinematic technique and film criticism has a limited appeal as subject matter, and Bergman's latest comedy is no more than a clever tour de force.

CHAPTER 12

Conclusion

I NGMAR BERGMAN'S reputation as an artist rests primarily on his work in the cinema. Surveys of his production often stress his isolated position in the contemporary Swedish film. To a large extent this is true. His younger colleagues—with the exception of Vilgot Sjöman—lack his preoccupation with metaphysical problems and have all striven toward a more immediate social consciousness. Nor has Bergman formed any "school" abroad. After he reached his international breakthrough in 1956, a certain Bergman impact could be seen in the French and Italian cinema. He probably helped launch the "New Wave" movement in France, which shares with him an interest in the inner life of man, but Bergman himself has denounced the nihilistic content of its films: "It is this emptiness that is so awful, this masturbation of the form that devours itself. Compare this with Fellini. He is a social critic, a sharp observer who—without appearing to do so—takes a violent stand precisely by showing the emptiness, the lack of love. But he puts it in relation to something. He has an alternative." [1]

When it comes to tracing Bergman's own development, critics have been more ingenious. He has been called Sweden's greatest French director because his early films bear obvious traces of the misty atmosphere and fatalistic philosophy of the Carné-Duvivier films of the thirties, and because a work like *Smiles of a Summer Night* has a certain likeness in theme and milieu to Réné Clair's *Les Règles du jeu*. But Bergman has also been praised as Sweden's greatest German director because of his expressionistic technique in *The Devil's Wanton* and *Wild Strawberries*. And finally, he has been mentioned as Sweden's greatest Russian film-maker because of his "exquisite pictorial sense." [2]

To a large extent Bergman is an autodidact in the cinema. During his formative years as a film-maker his "untrained" and impressionable mind would absorb impulses from all cinematic sources. But labels identifying him with the film art of a specific country are misleading; he has never followed a particular cinematic trend for very long, and his early films testify to his eclectic assimilation of previous and contemporary movements in the cinema. And in the final analysis one must even question most of the alleged foreign influence in his films. For instance, the lyrical (at times sentimental) preoccupation with young love and innocence, coupled with a fatalistic belief in its ephemeral nature, which sets the melancholy "French" mood of some of Bergman's early films, could just as well have originated in his intense interest in the plays of Hjalmar Bergman.

The German influence is also debatable. *Wild Strawberries* can be related to Strindberg's post-Inferno production rather than to German expressionistic films. In its nightmarish mood and internalized plot, the film also bears a resemblance to *The Phantom Carriage*,[3] the work in which Victor Sjöström introduced something new to cinematic art: "a tension in the relationships between human beings . . . and between people and nature, reflected in the mind of the leading character and projected in dreamlike sequences." [4] *The Devil's Wanton*, too, is in structure related to *The Phantom Carriage*, which has a complex pattern of flashbacks within flashbacks, while its mood is that of Sweden's literary forties: an atmosphere of existentialist *Angst*.

The aim of both *The Phantom Carriage* and *Wild Strawberries* is moral: they tell of the change of heart in an egotistical old man and of his integration into a community of love. Such an attitude is the very opposite of that found in German expressionistic films, which strive toward ghoulish mysticism and aim at creating a world of maniacs and phantoms. In addition, German expressionistic films were shot almost exclusively in studios, while Bergman's sense of background and locale is in keeping with Swedish film tradition; it was Sjöström and Stiller (as well as Griffith) who began to shoot pictures out-of-doors. Their lyrical devotion to nature—what Vernon Young has called "the epic pastoralism of Swedish film"—was a trait they in turn absorbed from Swedish neo-Romanticism of the 1890s.

As for the Russian influence on Bergman, there is no doubt that he shares with Russian film-makers an interest in "characterizing details, a human character study by way of faces and facial expressions, the pictorial montage." [5] On the other hand, Bergman did not have to go to the Russian cinema to find these traits; they are present in Stiller's films, which in many ways anticipated the works of Eisenstein. Both directors relegated cinematic values to the realms of painting, architecture, and music rather than to literature.

Bergman's first practical experience with film-making, his apprenticeship under Alf Sjöberg, brought him indirectly into contact with the Russian cinema. Sjöberg received fundamental impulses from Russian (rather than German) expressionism in both film and theater, and he was no doubt the main artistic guide for the young Bergman although certain aspects of Sjöberg's Russian-inspired expressionism—his somewhat abstracted montageship and his social pathos—were soon toned down in his disciple's works.

Thus, while it is possible to see traces in Bergman's work of a variety of foreign sources, all the way from Chaplin, Meliès, and Cocteau to Carné, Buñuel, and Hitchcock, it is undoubtedly in the Swedish film and theater that he is deeply rooted. He has not only paid homage to Alf Sjöberg as well as to the makers of silent Swedish films but has also acknowledged his literary dependence upon such playwrights as Almquist, Strindberg, and Hjalmar Bergman, all three of whom combine a strong sense for realistic detail and verisimilitude with the conception of human life as something fantastic, grotesque, or dreamlike.

Tentatively and as a summing up, the following characteristics, which Bergman's films share with earlier works in the Swedish cinema and theater, may be singled out:

1. A tendency to relate man to his surrounding landscape, coupled with an ambivalent conception of nature as a force to be loved and feared. At the same time as the characters feel an almost pantheistic rapport with nature, they recognize in it a barbarous force that reminds them of man's own atavistic instincts. The oscillation between the lyrical and the horrific in depicting man's reaction to nature can be led back to German Romanticism, which obtained a strong footing in Scandinavia in the first half of the nineteenth century. A fusion of idyl and gothic mystery is found in the early dramas of Carl Jonas Love Almquist (1793–1866); his best known play, *Amorina* (1839), was revived in the nineteen-forties by director Alf Sjöberg. The production was considered epoch-making and had a great impact upon a

whole generation of Swedish artists.[6] Bergman also encountered this nature dualism in the classic films of Sjöström and Stiller. Sjöström, in particular, identified strongly with Selma Lagerlöf, upon whose work he (and Stiller) based many of their films. Selma Lagerlöf substituted the mystique of folklore and legend for the neo-Platonic transcendentalism and gothic horror visions of earlier Swedish Romantics, but imposed upon her work a strong moralistic tone based upon Christian ethics.

2. *A moral approach to art.* In the cinema, Victor Sjöström (rather than Stiller, whose mind tended toward estheticism) would be Bergman's master in this respect. But also major Swedish playwrights like Strindberg, Hjalmar Bergman, and Pär Lagerkvist are moralists, and it could be their point of view that Bergman expresses when he states in an interview: ". . . the only thing we can and should deal with in dramatic form are the ethical subjects. . . . Our whole existence is built up around this concept that there are things we may do and other things we may not do, and it is these complications which we continually come in contact with during our entire life." [7]

3. *A predilection for the abstract pattern of the old morality play.* The Swedish dramatic and cinematic tradition makes generous use of stylized characters and symbolic actions. Bergman's dramatic figures, who frequently emerge as embodiments of ideas or rudimentary human attitudes, could be termed cinematic descendants of Strindberg's characters; not only in Strindberg's "dream plays" but also in his so-called naturalistic dramas, like *The Father* and *The Dance of Death,* the dramatis personae are stylized representatives of the male and female, engaged in elemental conflicts between the sexes or between Man and a godhead.

Central in the play production of Hjalmar Bergman, who adapted many of his works for the screen (some of them directed by Victor Sjöström), stands *Sagan* (*The Fairy Tale*), written in 1923 but neither published nor produced until 1942. This drama, the staging of which later became one of Ingmar Bergman's great triumphs as a theater director, is an interplay of fantasy and real life, a tension between people who represent beauty and unselfish love and those who personify wisdom and common sense. In Sune, the young spokesman for the world of fantasy (which is not merely a fabricated world but can be part of reality), Hjalmar Bergman depicts the *tainted* idealist, who wins love but not absolute goodness. Here we may have one of the prototypes for Ingmar Bergman's many imperfect seekers.

In Selma Lagerlöf's world as projected on the screen by Sjöström and Stiller, Bergman would find abstractionism set against a conventionally Christian background. The religious archetypes in Bergman's works—especially the frequent presence of the devil figure—which are no doubt part of his heritage as a pastor's son,[8] could easily fit into such films as *The Phantom Carriage* and *Gösta Berling*.

In spite of an emphasis on social realism in Swedish fiction of the thirties, abstractionism continued to have an impact through the works of Pär Lagerkvist. A decade later Stig Dagerman—the epitome of the literary mood at the time when Bergman began his career as a film-maker—made his debut as a playwright with the stylized, metaphysical drama *The Condemned* (*Den dödsdömde*), the production of which became one of the major theater events in Sweden during the nineteen-forties.

4. A fine sense of rhythm, manifesting itself in mood as well as cinematic technique (swift cutting, juxtaposition of long shots and close-ups); a feature that may be related not only to Stiller's precise feeling for musical counterpoint but also to what has been called "the noon wine syndrome" in Swedish art, a peculiar dualism in which "a cold radiance and crystalline gloom seem continually to convey a perilous balance between the light-dark extremities of human emotion." [9]

But Ingmar Bergman has not only echoed older Swedish filmmakers and men of the theater. His work has also a deeply personal foundation. Some critics even feel that his vision is too subjective and his symbolism beyond the reach of the spectator: "Bergman, like Cocteau, is an artist who presents us with his own private world of myth and illusion. Everything is there except the key to the last door of his Bluebeard's Castle." [10] Others, however, have pointed out that a private symbol is not necessarily devoid of objective meaning: "These [the symbols] may have some personal meaning to him . . . , but this is not so important as the fact that he chooses so effectively from such personal associations those that will project most awesomely to us the feelings the originals may have aroused in him. Actually, within a context of uncertainty his work has a strange clarity." [11]

Such diverse opinions notwithstanding, it is beyond dispute that Bergman has added new dimensions to the cinema as an art form. He has revived the concept of *l'auteur de cinéma,* such as the film industry had known it in the days of Meliès, and in his own right he is a creator of new forms. He has perfected the inward movement of the earlier Swedish film, and he has introduced new and daring aspects of the film medium: the use of natural sounds instead of dramatic music, and a refined handling of the close-up, which he rightly feels is a film-maker's most important means for freeing the cinema from its dependence upon the stage:

Our work in films begins with the human face. We can certainly become completely absorbed in the esthetics of montage, we can bring objects and still life into a wonderful rhythm, we can make nature studies of astounding beauty, but the approach to the human face is without doubt the hallmark and distinguishing quality of the film.[12]

What Bergman has done, in short, is to demonstrate that the film-maker, no less than the poet and playwright, can consistently use his medium as artistic self-expression. It may be no exaggeration when the American film critic Lewis Jacobs states that Bergman "stands today at the threshold of what may turn out to be a new artistic development of the medium, one as radical as Griffith's was in his day." [13]

Notes and References

Preface

1. Harry Schein, "Poeten Bergman," *BLM*, No. 9, (November, 1959), p. 352.
2. *Four Screenplays of Ingmar Bergman*, (New York: Simon & Schuster, 1960), p. xviii.
3. Vilgot Sjöman, *L 136*, (Stockholm: Norstedts, 1963), p. 22.
4. Quoted in Frederic Fleisher, "Early Bergman," *Encore*, No. 36, (March–April, 1962), p. 19.
5. Vilgot Sjöman's study *L 136* suggests that Bergman has often felt that "das Gewollte," his *willed ambition*, played a greater part in the conception of a work than it should. As of *Winter Light* (*Nattvardsgästerna*, 1963) he tries to avoid imposing his consciousness upon a script: "First I write down everything I know of the plot, in a long and involved way. Then I sink the iceberg and let only some of it float up to the surface." Sjöman, *L 136*, p. 191.
6. *Four Screenplays of Ingmar Bergman*, pp. xv–xvi.
7. Lionel Trilling, "Bergman Unseen," *The Mid-Century*, No. 20, (December, 1960), p. 5.
8. *Four Screenplays of Ingmar Bergman*, p. xvi.
9. Quoted in Bengt Idestam-Almquist, *Great Classics of the Swedish Cinema: The Stiller-Sjöström Period*, (Stockholm: The Swedish Institute, 1952), p. 32.
10. Quoted in Allardyce Nicoll, *Film and Theatre*, (New York: Thomas Y. Crowell Co., 1936), p. 120.
11. *Ibid.*, p. 121.
12. *Ibid.*, p. 48.
13. Hollis Alpert, "Bergman as Writer," *Saturday Review of Literature*, August 27, 1960, p. 22.
14. Lionel Trilling, "Bergman Unseen," *The Mid-Century*, No. 20, (December 1960), p. 6.
15. Pauline Kael, "Brooding, They Said," *The New York Times*, February 21, 1965.
16. "Såsom i en spegel. En intervju," *Chaplin*, No. 23, (November, 1961), p. 213.

CHAPTER 1

1. From an interview in *Filmnytt*, No. 6 (1950), p. 13.

2. "It is completely natural for artists to take from and give to each other, to borrow from and experience one another. In my own life, my great literary experience was Strindberg. . . . And it is my dream to produce *A Dream Play* some day. Olof Molander's production of it in 1934 was for me a fundamental dramatic experience." *Four Screenplays of Ingmar Bergman*, p. xix.

3. Quoted in Gunnar Oldin, "Ingmar Bergman," *The American-Scandinavian Review*, XLVII (Autumn, 1959), p. 142.

4. From a lecture in Uppsala on February 23, 1959. Quotation from a resumé in *Upsala Nya Tidning*, February 24, 1959.

5. Bengt Jahnson, "Bergmans avgång," *Dagen Nyheter*, November 28, 1965.

6. Quoted in Gunnar Oldin, "Ingmar Bergman," *The American-Scandinavian Review*, XLVII (Autumn, 1959), pp. 152–53.

7. Ingmar Bergman, "Self-Analysis of a Film-Maker," *Films and Filming*, September 24, 1956, p. 19.

8. *Time*, March 14, 1960, p. 62. (Cover story on Ingmar Bergman).

9. See Marianne Höök, *Ingmar Bergman*, (Stockholm: Wahlström & Widstrand, 1962).

10. Siegfried Kracauer, *From Caligari to Hitler*, (Princeton: Princeton University Press, 1947), p. 6.

11. Jean Béranger, "Renaissance du cinéma suèdois," *Cinéma 58*, No. 29, (July-August, 1958), p. 32.

12. Alan Cole, "Ingmar Bergman. Movie Magician," *New York Herald Tribune*, November 8, 1959.

13. Cf. Jörn Donner, *The Personal Vision of Ingmar Bergman*, (Bloomington: Indiana University Press, 1962), p. 212.

14. Ingmar Bergman, "A Page From My Diary," reprinted in a program distributed at the foreign showing of *The Virgin Spring*, (Stockholm: Svensk Filmindustri, 1960), n.p.

CHAPTER 2

1. I.e., the production that followed upon Strindberg's religious crisis in the mid-1890s, most notably such dramas as *A Dream Play* and the so-called "chamber plays" (e.g., *The Ghost Sonata*).

2. Quoted in Åke Runnquist, "Den demoniska silverpennan," *BLM*, No. 3 (March, 1948), p. 293.

In his book *L 136* Vilgot Sjöman relates an episode of devious Lagerkvist "influence": Bergman rejected a suggestion of possible

Lagerkvist traces in a sequence in *Winter Light*. Later the scene was cut, and Bergman motivated it by calling it "just bad Pär Lagerkvist." Sjöman, *L 136*, p. 37.

3. "Ingmar Bergman ser på film," *Chaplin*, No. 18 (March, 1961), p. 61.

4. Robert van Hijn: *van*, suggesting Swedish *fan* = devil; *Hijn*, suggesting Swedish *Hin* = the Evil One.

5. Åke Runnquist, "Den demoniska silverpennan," *BLM*, No. 3, (March, 1948), p. 294.

6. "Ingmar Bergman ser på film," *Chaplin*, No. 18 (March, 1961), p. 61.

7. *Ibid.*, p. 62.

CHAPTER 3

1. Statement by Ingmar Bergman in a program note at the Swedish première of *Torment*. (Stockholm: Svensk Filmindustri, 1944), n.p.

2. Lasse Bergström, *Skott i mörkret. Filmessäer*, (Stockholm: Wahlström & Widstrand, 1956), p. 6.

3. Jacques Siclier, *Ingmar Bergman*, (Paris: Editions Universitaires, 1960), p. 22.

4. Eric Ulrichsen, "Skepp till Indialand," *Det danske film-museum programblad*, n.d.

5. "Hamnstads slutscener togs först," *Göteborgs-Tidningen*, July 5, 1948.

6. Jacques Siclier, *Ingmar Bergman*, p. 29.

7. Cf. Peter Cowie, *Antonioni, Bergman, Resnais*, (Loughton, Essex: Motion Picture Publications, 1963), p. 53.

8. Eric Ulrichsen, "Ingmar Bergman and the Devil," *Sight and Sound*, XXVII (Summer, 1958), p. 226.

CHAPTER 4

1. Marianne Höök, *Ingmar Bergman*, p. 80.

2. Jacques Siclier, *Ingmar Bergman*, p. 53.

3. Comparison first suggested by Peter Cowie, *Antonioni, Bergman, Resnais*, p. 55.

4. The American title is ludicrous, suggesting the very opposite of Bergman's intentions. The literal title is "Summer Play."

5. Quoted in Jörn Donner, *The Personal Vision of Ingmar Bergman*, p. 80.

6. Gerd Osten, *Nordisk film*, (Stockholm: Wahlström & Widstrand, 1951), p. 45.

7. Marianne Höök, *Ingmar Bergman*, p. 77.

8. *Ibid.*, p. 75.

9. Cf. Jörn Donner, *The Personal Vision of Ingmar Bergman*, p. 85.

10. Harry Schein, "En ny Bergman," *BLM*, No. 9 (November, 1951), p. 714.

11. Eugene Archer, "The Rack of Life," *Film Quarterly*, No. 4, (Summer, 1959), p. 7.

12. *Ibid.*, p. 9.

13. Peter Cowie, *Antonioni, Bergman, Resnais*, p. 62.

14. Jean Collet, "Rêves de femmes," *Télé-Ciné*, No. 85 (October, 1959), p. 342.

15. Harry Schein, "Filmkrönika," *BLM*, No. 7 (September, 1955), p. 567.

16. See Jörn Donner, *The Personal Vision of Ingmar Bergman*, p. 123.

17. Hollis Alpert, "Style is the Director," *Saturday Review of Literature*, December 23, 1961, p. 40.

18. Quoted in Jean Béranger, "Rencontre avec Ingmar Bergman," *Cahiers du Cinéma*, No. 88 (October, 1958), p. 153.

19. Peter Cowie, *Antonioni, Bergman, Resnais*, p. 101.

20. *Ibid.*, p. 101.

21: Jörn Donner, *The Personal Vision of Ingmar Bergman*, p. 22.

CHAPTER 5

1. Cowie, *Antonioni, Bergman, Resnais*, p. 113.

2. *Ibid.*, p. 115.

3. Program note to *The Seventh Seal*, (Stockholm: Svensk Filmindustri, 1957), n.p.

4. Henry Hart, "The Seventh Seal," *Films in Review*, IX (March, 1959), p. 43.

5. "Philosophically, there is a book which was a tremendous experience for me: Eino Kaila's *Psychology of the Personality*. His thesis that man lives strictly according to his needs—negative and positive—was shattering to me, but terribly true. And I built on this ground." *Four Screenplays of Ingmar Bergman*, p. xxi.

CHAPTER 6

1. In an unpublished article Olle Sjögren mentions as possible Strindberg influences: a) The rendering of the jubilee festivities in Lund, perhaps inspired by the meeting of the four faculties in *A Dream Play* although, as Sjögren points out, the mood in Bergman's film is boredom rather than farce. b) The examination of Isak Borg, reminiscent of the Officer's testing in the multiplication table in *A Dream Play*. c) The Alman couple, tied to each other in Strindbergian love-hatred. d) The final scene, which points to the Hunter's description of an idyllic landscape in *The Great Highway*. e) The

Doppelgänger and Repetition themes, reminiscent of similar motifs in *To Damascus*.

2. Jacques Siclier, *Ingmar Bergman*, p. 148.

3. Walter Sokel, *Writer in Extremis*, (Princeton: Princeton University Press, 1962), p. 32.

4. One is reminded here of a scene in Act I of Stig Dagerman's play *The Condemned*. Petrus, the dying lawyer, relates a frightening experience: in a park he has just met an awesome-looking old man pushing a wheelbarrow, out of which dangled the limp arm of a dead man. Petrus felt compelled to pursue it.

5. Peter Cowie, *Antonioni, Bergman, Resnais*, p. 96.

6. Eugene Archer, "Wild Strawberries," *Film Quarterly*, XII (Fall, 1959), p. 44.

7. The script for *Wild Strawberries* seems in part to be based on an actual episode in Victor Sjöström's life when he went through a crisis similar to the one of Isak Borg in Bergman's film: "At the turn of the year 1915–16, Sjöström felt very depressed. He was dissatisfied with his life. He had not succeeded in making better motion picture art, which he had dreamed he would. . . . He was deeply unhappy, also for non-artistic reasons. His marriage to Danish actress Lili Beck had not gone well . . . and Sjöström's faith in life and in human nature had received a serious blow. . . . Sjöström bought a bicycle and started out into the country on a sentimental journey, to visit places where he—according to what he had heard—had lived with his parents when he was a child but where he had never been as a man. It was a strange journey. Little by little Sjöström's faith in man was built up again." Bengt Idestam-Almquist, *Classics of the Swedish Cinema: The Stiller-Sjöström Period*, pp. 47–48.

CHAPTER 7

1. To be discussed in Chapter 9, entitled "The Trilogy." Bergman's latest film to date, *Persona*, is also relevant in this context, but since it is conceived in the same spirit as the chamber plays it will be discussed with these.

2. Jörn Donner, *The Personal Vision of Ingmar Bergman*, p. 65.

3. Jacques Siclier, *Ingmar Bergman*, p. 84.

4. Eugene Archer, "The Rack of Life," *Film Quarterly*, No. 4, (Summer, 1959), p. 16.

5. Caroline Blackwood, "The Mystique of Ingmar Bergman," *Encounter*, No. 91 (April, 1961), p. 56.

6. Ingmar Bergman, "Det förbjudna. Det tillåtna. Det nödvändiga," *Vi på SF*, (April, 1957), n.p.

7. Stig Wikander, "Magiker eller frälsare," *Svenska Dagbladet*, January 4, 1959.

8. Carl-Erik Nordberg, "Det gåtfulla ansiktet," *Vi*, January 17, 1959, p. 14.

9. Vernon Young, "Bergman's The Magician," *The Art Film*, 1961, n.p.

10. Quoted in Peter Cowie, *Antonioni, Bergman, Resnais*, p. 32.

11. Jurgen Schildt, "Brev till Ingmar Bergman," *Vecko-Journalen*, April 16, 1958.

12. Cf. Hans Lindström, "Kommentar till 'Ansiktet'," *Upsala Nya Tidning*, January 15, 1959.

13. Source suggested by Marianne Höök, *Ingmar Bergman*, p. 142.

14. Georges Sadoul, "Ambigu dramatique," *Les Lettres Françaises*, October 8, 1959, p. 43.

15. A similar ambivalence in the artist's role in society is handled by Thomas Mann in *The Magic Mountain*.

CHAPTER 8

1. Marianne Höök, *Ingmar Bergman*, p. 146.

2. Ulla Isaksson, *The Virgin Spring*, (New York: Ballantine Books, 1960), p. vi.

3. Cf. Jörn Donner, *The Personal Vision of Ingmar Bergman*, p. 189.

4. Italics mine.

5. Jörn Donner, *The Personal Vision of Ingmar Bergman*, p. 189.

6. Colin Young, "The Virgin Spring," *The Art Film*, 1961, n.p.

7. Quoted in Donner, *The Personal Vision of Ingmar Bergman*, p. 193.

8. Peter Cowie, *Antonioni, Bergman, Resnais*, p. 98.

9. Isabel Quigly, "The Light that Never Was," *Spectator*, June 9, 1961, p. 839.

10. Robin Hood, "Jungfrukällan främst regikonst," *Stockholms-Tidningen*, February 9, 1960.

11. Ulla Isaksson, *The Virgin Spring*, p. vi.

12. Quoted in Sven Stolpe, "Jungfrukällan än en gång," *Aftonbladet*, February 26, 1960.

13. In his review of the film, Bengt Idestam-Almquist suggests that in this sequence Töre frees himself of his own lust for Karin. Robin Hood, "Jungfrukällan främst regikonst," *Stockholms-Tidningen*, February 9, 1960.

14. Marianne Höök, *Ingmar Bergman*, p. 151.

15. Quoted in Sven Stolpe, "Jungfrukällan än en gång," *Aftonbladet*, February 26, 1960.

16. William S. Pechter, "The Ballad and the Source," *The Kenyon Review*, XXIII (Spring, 1961), p. 334.

17. Statement quoted in Hollis Alpert, "Style is the Director," *The Saturday Review of Literature*, December 23, 1961, p. 40.

18. Norman S. Holland, "Bergman Springs Again," *The Hudson Review*, XIV (Spring, 1961), p. 110.

CHAPTER 9

1. Vilgot Sjöman, *L 136*, p. 10, footnote.
2. Göran Persson, "Bergmans trilogi," *Chaplin*, No. 40 (October, 1963), p. 228. Throughout this chapter I remain much indebted to this article.
3. Marianne Höök, *Ingmar Bergman*, p. 155.
4. From a conversation reported in Vilgot Sjöman, *L 136*, p. 28.
5. *Ibid.*, p. 28.
6. Sylvia Elmund, "Nattvardsgästerna—en kommentar till Jörn Donners filmkrönika," *BLM*, No. 3 (March, 1963), pp. 237–39, and Hans Nystedt, "Ingmar Bergman som Kristus och Tomas," *Svenska Dagbladet*, April 21, 1963.
7. Robin Wood, "Bergman's Winter Light," *Movie*, No. 10 (November, 1963), p. 233.
8. Göran Persson, "Bergmans trilogi," *Chaplin*, No. 40 (October, 1963), p. 229.
9. *Ibid.*, p. 238.
10. Vilgot Sjöman, *L 136*, pp. 29–30.
11. Göran Persson, "Bergmans trilogi," *Chaplin*, No. 40 (October, 1963), p. 228.
12. Torsten Manns, "Tystnaden," *Chaplin*, No. 40 (October, 1963), p. 240.
13. *Ibid.*, p. 241.
14. Margit Abenius, "Dagens debatt," *BLM*, No. 10 (December, 1963), pp. 820–22.
15. Jörn Donner, *The Personal Vision of Ingmar Bergman*, p. 231.
16. Statement quoted in Hollis Alpert, "Style Is the Director," *Saturday Review of Literature*, December 23, 1961, p. 41.

CHAPTER 10

1. Cf. Axel Liffner, "Hatade Bergman sin mor" *Aftonbladet*, October 30, 1966.
2. Ingmar Bergman, *Persona*, (Stockholm: P. A. Norstedt, 1966), p. 58.
3. *Ibid.*, pp. 10, 12.
4. Cf. Hans Nystedt, "Ingmar Bergman, religionen och rollerna," *Svenska Dagbladet*, November 19, 1966.

5. See Stig Algren, "Persona," *Idun-Veckojournalen,* December 2, 1966.
6. Ingmar Bergman, *Persona,* p. 85.
7. Cf. Jurgen Schildt, "Människan, maskerna och mästerskapet," *Aftonbladet,* October 19, 1966.

CHAPTER 11

1. Rune Waldecrantz, "The Swedish Film: A Personal Vision," *Augustana Swedish Institute Yearbook, 1964–65,* (Rock Island, 1965), p. 12.
2. Caroline Blackwood, "The Mystique of Ingmar Bergman," *Encounter,* No. 91 (April, 1961), p. 54.
3. Quoted in Marianne Höök, *Ingmar Bergman,* p. 109.
4. David Sylvester, "The Films of Ingmar Bergman," *The New Statesman,* October 18, 1958, p. 518.
5. Henry Hart, "Smiles of a Summer Night," *Films in Review,* VII (Summer, 1958), p. 243.
6. Peter Cowie, *Antonioni, Bergman, Resnais,* p. 78.
7. Quoted in Hollis Alpert, "Style Is the Director," *Saturday Review of Literature,* December 23, 1961, p. 40.
8. Peter Cowie, *Antonioni, Bergman, Resnais,* p. 82.
9. Ingmar Bergman, "Kära skrämmande publik," *SF Filmblad till Djävulens öga,* (Stockholm: Svensk Filmindustri, 1960), n.p.

CHAPTER 12

1. "Ingmar Bergman ser på film," *Chaplin,* No. 20 (May, 1961), p. 124.
2. Cf. Alan Cole, "Ingmar Bergman, the Movie Magician," *The New York Herald Tribune,* October 25, 1959.
3. Based on a novel by Selma Lagerlöf, Sjöström's version of *The Phantom Carriage (Körkarlen,* 1921)—Duvivier made another version in 1937 and Arne Mattson still another in 1955—is according to Chaplin "the best film ever made."
4. Bengt Idestam-Almquist, *Great Classics in the Swedish Cinema: The Stiller-Sjöström Period,* p. 30.
5. *Ibid.,* p. 12.
6. Cf. Rune Waldecrantz, *The Swedish Cinema,* (Stockholm: The Swedish Institute, 1960), n.p.
7. "Vågskvalp i bakvatten," *Chaplin,* No. 20 (May, 1961), p. 125.
8. "A child who is born and brought up in a vicarage acquires an early familiarity with life and death behind the scenes. Father performed funerals, marriages, baptisms, gave advice, and prepared sermons. The Devil was an early acquaintance, and in the child's mind there was a need to personify him. This is where my magic lantern

came in. . . . I can still remember . . . Red Riding Hood and the Wolf, and all the others. And the Wolf was the Devil, without horns but with a tail and a gaping red mouth, strangely real yet incomprehensible, a picture of wickedness and temptation on the flowered wall of the nursery." *Four Screenplays of Ingmar Bergman,* p. xiv.

9. Arlene Croce, "The Bergman Legend," *Commonweal,* March 11, 1960, p. 649.

10. John Gillet, "Films from Sweden," *International Film Annual,* (London & New York: 1959), p. 101.

11. Paul V. Buckley, "A Forceful Swedish Talent," *The New York Herald Tribune,* May 5, 1958.

12. Quoted in Hollis Alpert, "Style Is the Director," *Saturday Review of Literature,* December 23, 1961, p. 40.

13. Lewis Jacobs, *Introduction to the Art of the Movies,* (New York: The Noonday Press, 1960), p. 38.

Selected Bibliography

I. Books and Articles by Ingmar Bergman
WORKS IN SWEDISH

A. *Essays and Short Stories:*

"Det att göra film," *Filmnyheter*, No. 19–20 (December, 1954).
"En kortare berättelse om ett av Jack Uppskärarens tidigaste barn-domsminnen," *40–tal*, No. 3 (1944).
"Filmskapandets dilemma," *Hörde ni?*, No. 5 (1955).
"Fisken. Fars för film," *Biografbladet*, No. 4 (Winter, 1950–1951).
"Sagan om Eiffeltornet," *BLM*, No. 9 (September, 1953).
Untitled "anti-Bergman" article under pseudonym of Ernest Riffe, *Chaplin*, No. 18 (March, 1961).

B. *Plays and Screenplays:*

En filmtrilogi (Stockholm: Norstedts, 1963). Swedish edition of *Through a Glass Darkly, Winter Light,* and *The Silence.*
Jack hos skådespelarna, (Stockholm: Albert Bonniers, 1948).
Moraliteter, (Stockholm: Albert Bonniers, 1948).
Persona, (Stockholm: Norstedts, 1966).
Staden. Printed in *Svenska radiopjäser 1951*, (Stockholm: Sveriges radio, 1951).
Trämålning. Printed in *Svenska radiopjäser 1954* (Stockholm: Sveriges radio, 1954).

WORKS IN TRANSLATION
English:

Every Film Is My Last. Monograph, (Stockholm: The Swedish Institute, n.d.).
Four Screenplays of Ingmar Bergman, (New York: Simon & Schuster, 1960). Contains the scripts of *The Seventh Seal, Smiles of a Summer Night, Wild Strawberries,* and *The Magician.*
Wood Painting, Tulane Drama Review, VI (Winter, 1961).

French:

Oeuvres, (Paris: Robert Laffont, 1962). French edition of *Four Screenplays*, plus the scripts of *Illicit Interlude* and *The Naked Night.*

149

Une trilogie, (Paris: Robert Laffont, 1963). Scripts of *Through a Glass Darkly, Winter Light* and *The Silence.*

German:

Das Schweigen, Cinemathek 12 (Hamburg: Marion von Schröder Verlag, 1965). German edition of *The Silence.*
Das siebente Siegel, Cinemathek 7, (Hamburg: Marion von Schröder Verlag, 1963). German edition of *The Seventh Seal.*
Wie in einem Spiegel, Cinemathek 1, (Hamburg: Marion von Schröder Verlag, 1962). German edition of *Through a Glass Darkly.*
Wilde Erdbeeren, (Frankfurt: Suhrkamp, 1964). German edition of *Wild Strawberries.*

Italian:

4 film di Bergman, (Torino: Giulio Einaudi, 1961). Same scripts as in *Four Screenplays.*

II.   Books and Articles about Ingmar Bergman

The great bulk of Bergman scholarship is written in Swedish. Since few American and British students can be expected to know that language, only the most important Swedish books and articles have been listed here. For a more complete bibliography the student might consult Jörn Donner's *The Personal Vision of Ingmar Bergman,* (Bloomington: Indiana University Press, 1962), pp. 245–65.

Alpert, Hollis, "Show of Magic," *Saturday Review,* August 29, 1959.
———. "Bergman As Writer," *Saturday Review,* August 27, 1960.
———. "Style Is the Director," *Saturday Review,* December 23, 1961. Three articles based on interviews with Bergman.
Archer, Eugene, "The Rack of Life," *Film Quarterly,* XII (Summer, 1959). Analysis of Bergman's production up to and including *The Seventh Seal.*
Baldwin, James, "The Precarious Vogue of Ingmar Bergman," *Esquire,* (April, 1960). Reprinted in *Nobody Knows My Name,* (New York: The Dial Press, 1961). Notes from an interview with Ingmar Bergman.
Béranger, Jean, *Ingmar Bergman et ses films,* (Paris: Le Terrain-Vague, 1959). Survey of Bergman production up to 1959.
Blackwood, Caroline, "The Mystique of Ingmar Bergman," *Encounter,* XVI (April, 1961). A negative analysis of Bergman's reputation as a film-maker. The article contains several factual errors.
Burnevich, Jos, *Thèmes d'inspiration d'Ingmar Bergman,* (Brussels: Collection Encyclopedique du Cinema, No. 30, 1960). A dis-

cussion by a Jesuit priest of major themes in Ingmar Bergman's films.

Cole, Alan, "Ingmar Bergman, Movie Magician," *New York Herald Tribune,* October 24, November 1, November 8, 1959. A general presentation of Bergman's life and work.

Cowie, Peter, *Swedish Cinema* (London: Zwemmer, 1966). By far the best survey work of Swedish films. Cowie's discussion of Ingmar Bergman covers some 90 pages.

————. *Antonioni, Bergman, Resnais,* (New York: Barnes & Co., 1963). In part the best presentation of Bergman in English.

Croce, Arlene, "The Bergman Legend," *Commonweal,* March 11, 1960. Analysis of Bergman's role as film-maker with an attempt to relate him to Swedish art.

Chiaretti, Tommaso, *Ingmar Bergman,* (Rome: Canesi, 1964). Comprehensive study in Italian of Bergman's films, including his "trilogy."

Cuenca, Carlos Fernandez, *Ingmar Bergman,* (Madrid: Filmoteca Nacional de España, 1961). Spanish study of Bergman's life and his work up to 1960.

Donner, Jörn, *The Personal Vision of Ingmar Bergman,* (Bloomington: Indiana University Press, 1962). A complex but somewhat disorganized discussion of Bergman's work in the cinema.

Durand, Frédéric, "Ingmar Bergman et la littérature suédoise," *Cinéma 60, No. 47* (June, 1960). A superficial analysis of Bergman and Swedish literary tradition.

Fleisher, Frederic, "Early Bergman," *Encore,* No. 36 (March–April, 1962). Brief discussion of Bergman's theater plays.

Gillet, John, "Films from Sweden," *International Film Annual,* (London & New York: 1959). Survey of recent (1959) films from Sweden, including Bergman's *The Magician.*

Holland, Norman, "Iconography in *The Seventh Seal,*" *The Hudson Review,* XII (Summer, 1959). An analysis of the chess game in *The Seventh Seal.*

————. "A Brace of Bergman's," *The Hudson Review,* XII (Winter, 1959–1960). An analysis of *Brink of Life.*

————. "Bergman Springs Again," *The Hudson Review,* XIV (Spring, 1961). Analysis of *The Virgin Spring.*

Hopkins, Steven, "Bergman and the Critics," *Industria International,* (Stockholm: 1962). A critique of Bergman criticism.

Höök, Marianne, *Ingmar Bergman,* (Stockholm: Wahlström & Widstrand, 1962). A study in Swedish of Bergman's life and work. The book covers Bergman's production up to *The Silence.*

Idestam-Almquist, Bengt, *Classics of the Swedish Cinema: The*

Stiller-Sjöström Period, (Stockholm: The Swedish Institute, 1952). A discussion of the Age of Silent Film in Sweden.

Isaksson, Ulla, *The Virgin Spring,* (New York: Ballantine Books, 1960). English script of Bergman's film, with an introduction by the author.

Kael, Pauline, "Brooding, They Said," *New York Times,* February 21, 1965. Review of the paperback edition of *Four Screenplays of Ingmar Bergman.*

Lauritzen, Einar, *Swedish Films,* (New York: The Museum of Modern Art Film Library, 1962). Brief introduction to Swedish film art.

McGann, Eleanor, "The Rhetoric of *Wild Strawberries,*" *Sight and Sound,* XXX (Winter, 1960–61). Somewhat careless review of *Wild Strawberries.*

n. a., *Ingmar Bergman.* Monograph, *Centrofilm,* No. 33 (Winter, 1963). A series of Italian essays on Ingmar Bergman as a film-maker.

Nykvist, Sven, "Photographing the Films of Ingmar Bergman," *American Cinematographer,* (October, 1962). Brief essay by one of Ingmar Bergman's leading photographers.

Oldin, Gunnar, "Ingmar Bergman," *The American-Scandinavian Review,* XLVII (Autumn, 1959). A somewhat superficial introduction to Ingmar Bergman.

Oldrini, Guido, *La Solitudine di Ingmar Bergman,* (Parma: Ugo Guanda, 1965). An Italian discussion of the isolated position of Ingmar Bergman in the world of film-making.

Oliva, Ljubomir, *Ingmar Bergman,* (Prague: Orbis, 1966). Only major study of Ingmar Bergman from behind the Iron Curtain.

Pechter, William S., "The Ballad and the Source," *The Kenyon Review,* XXIII (Spring, 1961). Possibly the best English discussion of *The Virgin Spring.*

Persson, Göran, "Bergmans trilogi," *Chaplin,* No. 40 (October, 1963). A very perceptive study of Bergman's film trilogy.

Quigly, Isabel, "The Light That Never Was," *The Spectator,* June 9, 1961. British analysis of *The Virgin Spring.*

"Retrospective Bergman," *Cahiers du Cinéma,* No. 85 (July, 1958). French survey of Bergman's production, including summaries of *Wild Strawberries* and *Brink of Life.*

Rohmer, Eric, "Presentation d'Ingmar Bergman," *Cahiers du Cinéma,* No. 61 (July, 1956). One of the first international presentations of Ingmar Bergman.

Runnquist, Åke, "Bakom ansiktet," *BLM,* No. 9 (November, 1959). A comprehensive analysis of *The Magician.*

Sarris, Andrew, "The Seventh Seal," *Film Culture,* No. 19 (1959). Most comprehensive English analysis of *The Seventh Seal.*

Schein, Harry, "Poeten Bergman," *BLM,* No. 4 (April, 1957). A discussion of the visual impact of certain sequences in *The Seventh Seal.*

Siclier, Jacques, *Ingmar Bergman.* (Paris: Editions Universitaires, 1960). The best French discussion of Ingmar Bergman although it does not include an analysis of the "trilogy."

Simon, John, "Ingmar, The Image-Maker," *The Mid-Century,* No. 29 (December, 1960). A discussion of Bergman's visual talent in connection with the Mid-Century Book Club selection of *Four Screenplays of Ingmar Bergman.*

Sjöman, Vilgot, *L 136. Dagbok med Ingmar Bergman,* (Stockholm: Norstedts, 1963). Excerpts in English translation in Göran Palm's and Lars Bäckström's *Sweden Writes* (Stockholm: The Swedish Institute, 1965). A diary kept while Sjöman observed Bergman's shooting of *Winter Light.*

Spiegel Der, No. 44 (October, 1960). German cover story on Ingmar Bergman.

Steene, Birgitta, "Archetypal Patterns in Four Screenplays of Ingmar Bergman," *Scandinavian Studies,* XXXVII (February, 1965). A discussion of *The Seventh Seal, Wild Strawberries, Through a Glass Darkly,* and *Winter Light.*

Sylvester, David, "The Films of Ingmar Bergman," *New Statesman,* October 18, 1958. An appreciative discussion of Bergman's films up to 1958.

Theunissen, Gert H., *Das Schweigen und Sein Publikum,* (Köln: Verlag M. du Mont Schauberg, 1964). A discussion and survey of the reception of *The Silence* in Germany.

Time, LXXXV (March 14, 1960). Cover story on Ingmar Bergman.

Trilling, Lionel, "Bergman Unseen," *The Mid-Century,* No. 20 (December, 1960). A discussion of Bergman as a writer.

Ulrichsen, Eric, "Ingmar Bergman and the Devil," *Sight and Sound,* XXVII (Summer, 1958). A survey of Bergman's films up to 1958, with an emphasis on their metaphysical brooding.

Vermilye, Jerry, "An Ingmar Bergman Index," *Films in Review,* XI (May, 1961). Brief summaries of Bergman's films up to and including *The Virgin Spring.*

Waldecrantz, Rune, "The Swedish Film: A Personal Vision," *Augustana Swedish Institute Yearbook,* 1964–65, (Rock Island: 1965). Brief survey of the history of Swedish film.

————. *Swedish Cinema,* (Stockholm: The Swedish Institute, 1959). Expanded version of previous article.

Whitebait, William, "Bergman, the Illusionist," *The New Statesman,* February 17, 1961. A discussion of *The Magician.*

Wiskari, Werner, "Ingmar Bergman's *Silence,*" *The New York Times,*

December 1, 1963. A brief discussion of *The Silence* before its American première.

Wood, Robin, "A Toad in the Bread," *Definition*, No. 3 (1961). A somewhat Freudian discussion of *The Virgin Spring*.

Young, Vernon, "Bergman's The Magician," *The Art Film* (Los Angeles: UCLA, 1961). Most comprehensive American discussion of *The Magician*.

Index